W9-BSY-613

THE
READING
PROMISE

THE READING PROMISE

My Father and
the Books We Shared

Alice Ozma

Foreword by Jim Brozina

GRAND CENTRAL
PUBLISHING

NEW YORK   BOSTON

Grand Central Publishing
Hachette Book Group
237 Park Avenue
New York, NY 10017

www.HachetteBookGroup.com

Printed in the United States of America

First Edition: May 2011

10 9 8 7 6 5 4 3 2 1

Grand Central Publishing is a division of Hachette Book Group, Inc. The Grand Central Publishing name and logo is a trademark of Hachette Book Group, Inc.

The publisher is not responsible for websites (or their content) that are not owned by the publisher.

Library of Congress Cataloging-in-Publication Data
Ozma, Alice.
The reading promise : my father and the books we shared / by Alice Ozma. —First edition.
pages cm
ISBN 978-0-446-58377-0
1. Ozma, Alice—Books and reading.   2. Brozina, James—Books and reading.   3. Books and reading—United States.   4. Books and reading—Psychological aspects.   5. Oral reading.   6. Fathers and daughters—United States—Biography.   I. Title.

Z1003.2O96 2011
028'.9—dc22

2010046510

ACKNOWLEDGMENTS

To the three people who got the ball rolling—Cindy Vitto, Barbara Baals, Mike Winerip—you have no idea how you have changed my life. Thank you from the bottom of my heart.

My lovely and loving agent, Jennifer Gates: you are like no one else I have ever met. Everything about working with you makes me happy, and everything you do to help makes the project that much better. I could not have gotten any luckier. You are absolutely amazing.

To my ridiculously talented editor, Karen Kosztolnyik: thank you for believing that a twenty-two-year-old recent college grad could and *should* write a memoir without a ghostwriter! You took a huge gamble on my behalf, and I hope it pays off. I have so much respect for you, and for what you've done with my work. We sensed a connection in just a twenty-minute meeting for a reason: we knew this was right.

Everyone who is portrayed, however inaccurately,

ACKNOWLEDGMENTS

including: my father, my mother, my sister, Dan, Nathan, Brittany, Teece, Steph, and many more: please forgive me if I got anything wrong, and know how much I appreciate you. And double thanks to three people who had to listen to most of my complaining as I slugged through this: Dan, Steph, and Kath. I trust your judgment and your heart. I owe you all a trip to the zoo.

Big hugs to Holly Capertina, Don Kopreski, Kathy Procopio, and Donna Cedermark, Jesse Zuba (Rowan University, you are making a big mistake if you let him get away!), Nathan Carb, Evan Roskos, Glen Odom, Cathy Parrish, everyone at GCP, read-aloud godfather Jim Trelease, Jeanne Birdsall, the Lemire family, Nikki Jones, Adam Jordan, Adam Chazen, and Ryan S. Hoffman (you truly are a genius). Kisses to the Brozinas, Sandones, and Angelucci-Donofrios, and Lemires. Grammom and PopPop and my personal hero Brett Fauver—always missing you. All my love to Bill and Jane Thurman, and full-speed ahead with Read Aloud Chattanooga! Special thanks to Kevin Dixon for his work on my website (makeareadingpromise.com, if you were absolutely dying to know) and photographers Ryan Collerd and Alex Forster. Fond remembrances to *Venue Magazine*, my Pub Suite pals, my TVM casts, Angelo's Diner, and Laurel Hall Room 210. Couldn't have done it without string cheese, juice boxes (my cure for writer's block!), and LUSH Cosmetics' Dorothy bubble bars (and yes, I am mentioning the product specifically in hopes that you will bring it back!). Brian and Rabbi, you are as peerless as felines come. Thanks

ACKNOWLEDGMENTS

for sitting outside with me when I wrote on the porch. Go
Phils!

And to my father, who has promised to never read this
book because it is embarrassingly mushy, remember the words
we will dance to at my wedding: "God only knows what I'd
be without you."

For Avant, Prospectus, and literary magazines everywhere filled with nerdy, wonderful kids—there's hope for us yet.

FOREWORD

by Jim Brozina (Alice's dad)

One warm night in the summer of 1998 I returned from taking a friend and her daughter to a concert in Philadelphia to find my own daughter Alice hopping up and down in the driveway like a madwoman, waving her arms and screaming. Since it was nearly midnight, I thought that something terrible must have happened, so I stopped the car and jumped out. She was shouting, "What are you doing? Look at the time! Look at the time!" Then it struck me. I had completely forgotten about our reading streak! We went inside, grabbed our book, and started our night's reading posthaste.

Months before, in an effort to stave off the end of my time reading aloud to Alice, fearing she might outgrow it, we had made a pact that I would read aloud to her every night. Never one to use small measures, Alice had boldly stated that our streak should last for one thousand nights. I was taken aback by this, since in the course of a thousand nights, I felt that something was bound to go wrong and that it would be a practical impossibility. However, as a parent and teacher, I felt that my role should be to encourage and not discourage the aspirations of children. Just the same, the idea of a thousand nights did make my head spin.

As this story will tell you, our streak went on for many nights after that. Through all sorts of turmoil and circumstance we persevered until at last the streak ended almost nine years later. Since Alice and I are both people who do not look for precedent in anything we do, it only seemed a little bit odd that we spent a part of each day reading together from the time she was nine until the summer of her eighteenth year.

To keep our streak alive, there were some days when our reading started at twelve midnight and some days when we began at an ungodly hour of the morning. There were many times when I had to wake her up from a sound sleep. There were times when she (cautiously) had to awaken me. Neither of us ever complained about these circumstances. We were committed to doing this, and we were not going to allow any sort of inconvenience to stand in our way. Nothing that lasts has been accomplished without effort. The things that we are most proud of took quite a lot to achieve.

After our readings I would often ask Alice about her day and what was going on in her life. This became a natural way for us to keep in touch.

Largely, our readings came from the books that were delivered to my school through the three book fairs that I was able to hold for the students each year in my position as a school librarian. From each fair I would bring home a collection of titles that the two of us would mull over, reading sections from each until we had hit on the group of books that would serve our purpose.

Once started, a reading streak can be a hard thing to stop. The only thing that stopped us was when she moved away from home almost nine years after we began.

If you want to start your own reading streak, you should begin by taking your child to your local public library, where the two of you can look through the stacks for books that would fit your reading desires. When either of you find something, show it to the other. Let your child overrule your choices if he or she chooses, but be hesitant about rejecting those your child is excited about. Remember, this is being done *by* you but *for* him or her.

When you have accumulated as many books as will serve your purpose for now, check them out and take them home. Your child will be hopping with excitement as he or she anticipates the many good nights of reading ahead. As time goes along, you will both begin to identify favorite authors and series. Some of these you will want to return to again and again. You may consider purchasing the most popular from your local bookstore or through the many booksellers online. These treasures can be passed on from generation to generation. What greater gift to your descendants yet unborn than the love of books and reading?

My love of reading aloud began when I was very young. My mother, who did not have use of a car during the day as my father took it to work, would walk my brother and me to the local library (a distance of a mile and a half each way), where we were each allowed to check out two books. One was to be read on our own; the other she would read to us.

If you have been read to as a child, you are much more likely to read to your own children when they come along. Create a family tradition that can be passed on.

The greatest gift you can bestow upon your children is your time and undivided attention. As the years advance, you may reflect upon your life and see that in some areas, you have regrets about what you took to be a priority. No one will ever say, no matter how good a parent he or she was, "I think I spent too much time with my children when they were young."

Children are not easily fooled. They can tell where a parent's priorities are. When my wife left me I did not seek out companionship for more than six years. I wanted the girls to be absolutely sure that I would be there for them. If one parent moves out and the other is out on the town each night, where does that leave them? I guess they would have to think "Mom's got her new man, Dad has his new girl, but who has us?"

In 1985, the Commission on Reading, funded by the U.S. Department of Education, declared, "The single most important activity for building the knowledge required for eventual success in reading is reading aloud to children." Both reading in school and at home were encouraged. The conclusion the panel reached was, "It is a practice that should continue throughout the grades."

As I recall my own years as a student there was only one teacher who read aloud to us, and that was when I was a senior in high school. Mr. Frank Duffy read to us, with great relish, the play *Macbeth* by William Shakespeare. At the time the other students and I thought that he was goofing off and that he must be too lazy to really teach us anything. A couple of weeks into his reading we could hardly wait to hear what happened next. Everyone sat leaning over in his or her chair to catch every word. If any of the other students started talking while Mr. Duffy was reading, they were quickly told to be quiet and identified as real fools.

The end result of his taking time to read to us instead of having us read it to ourselves was that I have retained a lifetime interest in Shakespeare's works. What good would it have done if Mr. Duffy had taught this in the usual fashion so that when finished we would hope never to hear the name William Shakespeare again?

I doubt that Alice will tell you this in her story, but she was one of only three (out of over three hundred) students in her eighth-grade class to score "advanced proficient" in the reading section of her state test. At the time our reading streak was more than four years along. She had the highest PSAT in her class when she was in the eleventh grade. At that time our streak was in its seventh year. And she won two first-place awards in national writing competitions while a senior in high school, by which time we had been reading more than eight years without a miss.

All this has certainly not made Alice a dull girl. I think in everyone's life there is an incident that defines them, that shows their character and what they are made of. I never made or wanted Alice to take a job while in school; I think those days should be reserved for learning and having fun. There is plenty of time for the workaday world in the years to come, and I made enough through my work at the schools to provide what was necessary for both of us. Alice was free to do as she pleased in her spare time. She took it upon herself to write a play called *Tiny* and organized other talented teens to help her put this play on at one of my schools during summer vacation.

Other than providing the money she would need for costumes and incidentals, I had no role in this except as the adult in attendance. For her players she used students from my school who had volunteered to take part in her production. These students ranged from the second to the fifth grade. None had ever taken part in an adventure such as this. My school has always had a poverty rate of 88 percent or above. She could have chosen the more affluent school that she had attended as a child, which was located near our home, but it was her purpose to bring this sort of activity to children who had never experienced such things before.

Over forty students returned permission slips, which were very specific about what would be required of the actors as far as rehearsal times and dates. Less than half of her potential thespians attended the first rehearsal. The one who had shown the most potential in tryouts quit when she found that she had not been given the female lead. It was all downhill from there.

At play practice attendance was rarely more than half the

players who were scripted for parts that day, and those who came often arrived late. Her patience was sorely tested as key players would stop attending rehearsals for days at a time with no notice or reason. Her script had to be redone again and again as she dropped roles or combined them to meet the number of players she could count on being at practice. Those who had dropped out would sometimes return after a week and want their parts back.

I was heartsick at watching what was going on and what stress Alice was forced to work under to make this play a reality. Never once did Alice lose her temper or give way to despair. I hated to bring the subject of the play up with her in our spare time as I did not want my trepidations to overly influence her. I truly think that what she went through would have tested the patience of a saint and broken a man stronger than Ahab, but day after day Alice would regroup herself and refocus upon what could still be done instead of what had been lost.

The conclusion was a play that would have done a high school theater department proud. And she did another play the following year to similar results. Caring, confidence, and optimism define her. I have never known her to commit a mean-spirited act or to even think of putting herself ahead of others.

Before I had any children I used to say, "When they come along I will not speak to them until they are sixteen, and then I will tell them to get a job." Holding them in my arms made me rethink that idea. I have discovered very little in life that I am adept at doing. I cannot fix your car, repair your roof, or even drive a nail straight. However, I have given everything I have to being a father, and I happily stand back to see the results.

If a child sees something in a parent that that child aspires to, he or she will copy that parent and be content. If children feel that a parent is living a life that shows compassion and understanding, patience and love, that child will not have to reach a stage of rebellion against that parent. Why rebel against someone who has listened to you and wants to help you fulfill your dreams? A parent who has proven time and again that the growth and happiness of his or her children is priority number one does not have to worry about where those children are heading in life. They will be sensitive and productive members of society for as long as they live.

This story is by and about one such girl.

THE
READING
PROMISE

CHAPTER ONE

Day 1

"I am terribly afraid of falling, myself," said the Cowardly
Lion, *"but I suppose there is nothing to do but try it. So get
on my back and we will make the attempt."*
                                    —L. Frank Baum, *The Wonderful Wizard of Oz*

It started on a train. I am sure of it. The 3,218-night reading marathon that my father and I call The Streak started
on a train to Boston, when I was in third grade. We were
reading L. Frank Baum's *The Tin Woodman of Oz*, the twelfth
book in the beloved Oz series, a few hours into our trip. The
woman across the aisle turned to us and asked why my father
was reading to me on a train. We simply told her that this was
what we always did—he had been reading to me every night
for as long as I could remember, ever since we read *Pinocchio*
when I was four. Being on vacation didn't make much of a
difference. Why not read? Why not always read?

But her surprise made us think. If we were going to read

on vacation anyway, how hard could it be to make reading every night an official goal? I suggested to my father that we aim for one hundred consecutive nights of reading, and he agreed to the challenge. This is how I remember it.

If you ask my father, though, as many people recently have, he'll paint an entirely different picture.

"Lovie," he tells me, as I patiently endure his version of the story, "you're cracked in the head. Do you want to know what really happened or are you just going to write down whatever thing comes to mind?"

Lovie, as I'm sure you can guess, is not my real name. Alice is, but only sort of. My full name is Kristen Alice Ozma Brozina, but I don't care for Kristen. Alice and Ozma are names my father chose from literature, names I would later choose for myself. It's a decision that took a long time, but one I'm very happy I made. Those names always felt like my real names to me, as I'll explain later. Also, Lovie is not the affectionate pet name you might think it is. As are all things in my father's vocabulary, it is a reference to something—this time it's Mr. Howell's nickname for Mrs. Howell on *Gilligan's Island.* My father never calls me by my name; Lovie is his most commonly chosen alternative. But when I drop something, or forget something, or do any of the silly things we all manage to do on a regular basis, "Lovie" is often followed by phrases such as "you nitwit!"

"So tell me then," I say, standing in his doorway as he gets ready to run errands.

"Well, when did Mom leave?" he asks.

"I was ten."

"All right, so 1997 it started. The Streak was a year old when she left."

"And what were we reading?"

"Well," he says thoughtfully, "it had to be an Oz book. That's what we were into around that time. I wanted to try other things, but you were set in your ways."

So far, we agree. But I know this won't last long.

"We were on the bed, we'd just finished reading," he says, "and I was fearing the Curse of Mr. Henshaw."

"What is that curse?"

"*Dear Mr. Henshaw* was the book I was reading to Kathy when she asked me to stop reading to her," he says in an almost whisper.

It is clear that this memory, though nearly two decades old, still troubles him. My sister was in fourth grade when she said she no longer wanted my father to read to her. It seemed childish to her, especially since she was already reading novels on her own. But it wasn't so easy for my father. He was an elementary school librarian, and reading to children was what he liked to do best. And maybe next to being a father, it's also what he does best. His soothing voice and rehearsed facial expressions have won over thousands of children throughout his career. They won me over, too, but I was already on his side.

"For some time, I'd been planning to suggest to you that we do a streak, because then at least you'd be a little older when we stopped reading together. I brought it up, and honest to Pete, I thought you were going to say we should read a hundred nights in a row!" He laughs as he recalls this. I don't laugh because I think I did suggest a hundred nights in a row. Initially.

"No," he continues, "Right away you said, 'Let's do one thousand!' And I had to pretend to be enthusiastic, of course, but I wasn't too optimistic. One thousand nights is a long time."

I have to stop him there. None of this sounds right to me. First I remind him that our goal had been one hundred nights. When we reached that goal, however, and celebrated with a pancake breakfast at the local greasy spoon, we decided to set a new goal. We skipped the discussions of lower options, from two hundred to five hundred, and ultimately decided to try for one thousand nights. I tell him this, but he just shakes his head. When I try to explain that The Streak actually began on the train, he cuts me off.

"Ah, the Curious Incident of the Train in the Nighttime!" he says, adapting the title of one of our favorite Sherlock Holmes stories.

"I remember that part clearly," he continues, "because I never miss an opportunity to brag about what a good father I am. We were on the train to Boston, going up to see the sights for a weekend, and the woman next to us said how sweet it was that I was reading to you. I told her right away that we were on a streak, forty nights in! I was pleased with myself, absurdly pleased with myself, pleased as a peacock to have made it forty nights."

We both laugh this time, but I am laughing partly because I know he is wrong. The train was the first night. Obviously.

The thing is, no matter how many times we are asked, we can never get this story straight. We agree on a few of the details, but I was very young and he is getting older. Some memories blend together with others, and our individual versions of how The Streak started change so often, it is nearly impossible to come to any sort of agreement. We can't even remember when we started calling it The Streak, or whose idea it was to do so. If we knew it would eventually reach over thirty-two hundred nights and span almost nine years, from elementary school to my first day of college, we might have taken notes in the beginning. Years passed before we even started keeping track of the books we read during Read Hot (pronounced "Red Hot"—another term for our nightly addiction, phrasing we found in *The Great Gilly Hopkins*).

Just because we didn't know how it would end, though, didn't mean we took our Streak lightly. Our rules were always clear and firm: we had to read for at least ten minutes (but almost always much more) per night, every night, before midnight, with no exceptions. It should come from whatever book we were reading at the time, but if we were out of the house when midnight approached, anything from magazines to baseball programs would do. The reading should be done in person, but if the opportunity wasn't there, over the phone would suffice. Well, just barely. I could always hear the annoyance in my father's voice when I called to inform him that I was sleeping at a friend's. He'd sigh and put down the phone, and I'd wait for him to go get our book. Sometimes, he'd ask me to call back in ten minutes.

"I haven't even preread it yet!" he'd protest. He insisted on rehearsing (and with more adult books, sometimes censoring) our reading ahead of time.

We remember details from later in The Streak better, both because they are more recent and because our record was becoming more impressive. Once we reached over a thousand nights, close calls and readings at quarter to midnight became more nail-biting issues. Of course we both remember how it eventually ended. That's the sort of event even my father can't forget, an event we dreaded for years. To get there, though, we need a beginning, and frankly I don't know what that beginning is.

I think I was leaning against him, in the crook of his arm, with my head on his chest, as our train to Boston sped past houses and schools and baseball fields that became colorful blurs. We were already dedicated to L. Frank Baum and the Oz books—in fact, we were reading the entire series for the second, or maybe third, time. My father loved Baum's take on leadership and women, not to mention his spot-on, frank humor that made us laugh a little harder every time we reread something. I liked the wonderful descriptions of beautiful places, like palaces and magnificent dining rooms filled with people and good food. Whenever we stayed in a hotel, which we were about to in Boston, I wondered if it was like the palace of Glinda or Rinkitink. That night, as my father read the description of the palace in the Emerald City, with its marvelous banners and gem-encrusted turrets, I squirmed eagerly in my seat, excited to get to the Marriott and check in.

I review this, and my father shakes his head.

"That's how I remember it," my father insists, after repeating his story of the beginning, now for the third time today, the details varying just a bit each time. But then he sighs.

"Problem with my remembrances, though," he admits, "is that they're always so goofed up."

I sit for a minute, comparing my notes on both versions of the story, seeing what they have in common. I am about to begin my argument once more, since simply repeating something over and over again sometimes convinces my dad that I am right (or at least wears him out). He knows I'm getting riled up, though, because his back is already to me as I'm about to begin my diatribe.

"I'm going to go look for treasures in the coat closet," my father says, heading down the stairs.

I'm not sure if this is a saying I'm expected to know or a literal plan, but it's apparent that the conversation is over. I didn't think we'd come to an agreement, anyway.

But this is how I remember it.

CHAPTER TWO

Day 38

"I can swim," said Roo, "I fell into the river, and I swimmed. Can Tiggers swim?"

"Of course they can. Tiggers can do everything."

—A. A. Milne, *The House at Pooh Corner*

Seated at the center of Benjamin Franklin Memorial Hall in Philadelphia is a twenty-foot-tall statue of the man himself, looking a bit world-weary but still curious. I stood in front of him, a familiar face after years of membership at the Franklin Institute, but I looked past him; today, we were watching the sky.

At the center of the domed ceiling, eighty-two feet above our heads, a man was hanging with one arm from a red ribbon, swaying softly like a wind chime in the breeze. The room was silent—or at least I was. The latter was rare; my father smiled with surprise. The strange man's muscles, visible through his bright leotard, pulsed and contracted. Even eighty feet below him, I could see sweat dropping from his forehead. But his face stayed perfectly still. His smile, distant and serene, was unmistakably rehearsed. To me, that made it even better. I loved showmanship. He was not a child trying acrobatics for fun. He was a professional, going to work as usual, executing his moves, if not with joy, with precision and grace. He was being paid to create beauty, and he was doing it well.

"Is this why we came here?" I asked. We were members at a slew of Philadelphia museums and visited them every Saturday, but today we were early to the Franklin Institute. He nodded.

I saw the connection, even if my father hadn't intended one. Since we'd started our Streak just a few short weeks ago, it had felt like we were in the middle of a balancing act. What we were doing was beautiful, of course, but it was difficult. Sometimes I was tired, really tired, like last Saturday when we got back from a day trip to Baltimore so late that I'd barely been able to keep my eyes open. I struggled my way through my father's reading of the final pages of *James and the Giant Peach*, and then made him reread those pages the next night, because I thought I'd dreamed them. But really, I hadn't—there was just something about Roald Dahl books that made everything seem like a dream. The vivid colors, the underlying darkness that sometimes hinted at despair. The ending seemed just a bit too happy to fit the rest of the book, but I wasn't one to complain about a happy ending.

"Would you ever do that?" my father asked, pointing a finger to show me just how high up the man in the strange outfit really was. I replied without even taking my eyes off of the man.

"Of course," I said. "Who wouldn't?"

"Plenty of people. This man knows what he's doing, but it's still risky. Are you sure you would go up there? What if you fell? You'd crack your head open. Your brains would go mish-mash splish-splash all over the marble, and they'd ask me to clean it up."

I looked at the man in the sky. He seemed to be hard at work, but tireless. The movements came as fluidly twenty minutes into the routine as they did in the first seconds, if not more so. I looked at the hundred or more people standing beside us, looking up.

"If I died," I said finally, cheerfully, "everybody would be watching me."

He laughed. We stood for a few more minutes with our necks craned upward. The more I thought about it, the more I couldn't decide if we were all cheering for the man or secretly waiting for him to fall. Would it be such a bad way to die, though, with a crowd of people watching you do what you loved?

But then I imagined what it would be like to have people watching you do *everything* you loved. We loved to read, and The Streak was going well so far, in the sense that we were enjoying ourselves and we hadn't missed a night. But I liked that it was private, something we did at home with no one watching, something that no one one knew about. I hadn't even told my friends yet. I was confident that we could make it to one hundred nights—it even sounded easy. But my father was less sure, and that made me nervous. At least no one had to see us if we fell. Not like this man. If he fell, everyone would see. He'd die doing what he loved, yes, but everyone would see him fall. Not that it really seemed like he might. He was working hard and sweating profusely, but he knew what he was doing. Like us.

I noticed a small contraption up there with him suspended from the highest point of the dome—a shiny silver thing like a miniature airplane. It fascinated me. At first I thought it was just a theatrical set. He was playing a character, maybe a pilot who decided to pause his plane midair and jump out to hang from the clouds. But then I noticed that the plane too was swaying, only much more softly than the man, a motion hardly noticeable but somehow hypnotic. My eyes shifted from the man to the plane. I was waiting for something to happen, but I wasn't sure what. Was the plane going to fly? And after watching a man dangle over our heads on a hand-kerchief, would flight really be so impressive?

A flash of color in the miniature windows. Someone, or something, was inside. The routine seemed to be nearing an end, but the man reached for the door. A woman, dressed in beautiful peacock colors, unfolded herself from a tiny seat and sprung to meet him. I gasped. Was she up there all along? Why did he make her wait in that tiny plane, wound up like thread, while he had the whole ceiling to explore? It seemed a little selfish. More than anything, though, it was foolish; she was absolutely beautiful.

She danced with him, a silent and intense duet. When she hung from his hand, not once but three times throughout the routine, I saw that she trusted him. I wouldn't have, if he'd kept me in a box while everyone was watching him. But when they finished, I clapped. For her.

We headed to eat our lunch, peanut butter sandwiches from home, in the High Place. It was our secret spot, a set of stairs hidden in plain sight at the top of a staircase overlooking the atrium. The High Place was perfect for people watching, which we both loved. Distracted by a boy yo-yoing as we mounted the stairs, I tripped on my shoelaces.

"You clumsy she-ape!" my dad said affectionately, as he helped me to my feet.

"They'd no sooner get you up on that plane than you'd be tearing out of the sky face-first. I wouldn't have time to catch you, you know. Even if I did, you would crush me."

"I could do it," I said after he handed me my sandwich. I tried to pick the chunks out of the chunky peanut butter he insisted we eat.

"I mean, the woman up there was much better than the man," I continued. "It comes naturally to us."

I knew I had him there. My father was and is a devout feminist, if for no other reason than having two daughters. Female leaders were endlessly impressive to him. At this point in The Streak, we still hadn't gotten much further than rereading the Oz books. Those lovely female rulers, level-headed and kind (not to mention beautiful), were some of the first literary friends we'd made together. He applauded strong women, especially those with wits and a little sass. Even though I was regularly wearing my shirts backward and had recently cut off one of my eyebrows with the kitchen scissors, he was sure that I was capable of great things, as all women are. I rattled on.

"Yes, the woman was really the whole act. The man didn't

know what he was doing until she got there. The man was just sweating and spinning. She pulled it all together."

We took a moment to congratulate ourselves on our elevated seating and strong people-watching skills when we were able to spot, far across the room and behind some large signs, the trapeze artist himself, taking a new wardrobe out of a closet. To this day I do not know why a science museum hired an acrobat to dance across their ceiling, but they must have been impressed with his work, because he seemed to be preparing for a second show.

"I'll go talk to him," my father said.

I shrugged and continued picking at my sandwich. I hated chunky peanut butter almost more than I hated the way the sandwiches got mushy and sweaty after being wrapped in tinfoil and left at the bottom of our canvas travel bag for hours. And I still had not been able to convince my father that the bread on peanut butter and jelly sandwiches was not typically buttered, least of all heavily and on both sides. I had just decided to try to suck the jelly out and leave the rest of the lumpy mess for him to tackle when my father returned, smiling.

"Well," he said, as he hoisted himself back up to the seat, "It looks like you might get your chance."

Thinking he meant that we were going to eat in the museum's cafeteria for once, my dimples creased my sticky cheeks. I sat up a little straighter.

"Really?"

"Yes," he said, "It's all settled. I just talked to that man, he seems like a great guy, and he was worried sick because his wife's having some kind of gut pains. He thinks she might not be able to make the next show. Well, I told him right away that you'd already made cameos in two high school plays, and you're great in front of a crowd, and not scared to go up at all. He was so relieved! He's checking to see if they have a costume in your size. If they don't, I guess you'll have to go up in your street clothes."

I looked at my faded T-shirt. Many of the embroidered green stars were now hidden under globs of purple jelly. But this was not my main concern.

"Did he really say that?" I asked cautiously. My father could keep a great straight face. This could be a joke.

"Well, of course he was a little surprised when I told him you were nine. But once he heard about all your experience, and how great you are in the spotlight, I think he calmed down. Really, what choice does he have?"

He shook his head like it was a done deal.

I considered. Yes, I had been excited to go up, ready and willing, but I hadn't expected to go up without practice. This man obviously had lots of practice; he could do the routine all while keeping that same frozen smile. I needed a frozen smile, and that would take time—at least a few hours. If my father could insist, as he always did, that he needed time to practice reading a simple chapter from a book before sharing it with me, a quick rehearsal before risking my life seemed warranted.

"When is the next show?"

My father checked his watch.

"One," he replied, and then pointed at my sandwich. "So you'd better shovel it in."

The idea of eating, let alone "shoveling in" the mushy mess before me made me queasy.

"I don't think I'm ready," I said, "I need practice."

"He said he'd talk you through the whole routine before you start. It sounded pretty easy. And remember, the woman came out later on. You can watch him while he performs the second time and pick up tips. Get an idea for how he does it."

"What if I can't fit in that tiny plane?"

"You're a little thing," he replied, "she's a full-grown adult. If she can fit, you can fit."

He ate in silence for a few minutes. I slid my sandwich behind me and rustled through the bag until I found some cheese crackers, which I munched thoughtfully.

"Eat with your mouth closed!" my father barked after my first bite. Open-mouthed chewing was one of his biggest annoyances. "You can hang by one hand in front of a hundred people or more, but you can't hold your lips shut while you eat cheese crackers?"

I held my lips shut and continued thinking. I wasn't scared to go up if I knew what I was doing, and I could figure it out quickly enough, but I needed at least a dress rehearsal on the ground before I attempted the real thing. How could two adults, two men with jobs and wives (even if my mother and father were rapidly losing interest in each other) and an interest in science museums, expect a child to perform acrobatics midair without at least a quick dress rehearsal? It was absurd. I wouldn't do it. I'd decided.

"There he is!" my father shouted, as the performer walked by again, this time in a different costume. "I'll go talk to him. Finish your sandwich before I take it from you!"

He headed down the stairs and disappeared into the crowd, which was much thicker now that school groups were flooding the atrium for lunch. I slid down from my perch, tinfoil-wrapped mess in hand, and scraped all but a few crumbs into the nearest trash can. As any picky-eating, low-appetite, food-wasting kid knows, a clean plate is too obvious. You have to leave a few crumbs, and you have to have some on your face. I had that covered. I settled back into my seat just as my dad was approaching again.

"No luck," he called, shaking his head as he climbed back up. "They couldn't find a costume in your size that didn't have sweat stains on it, and then his wife got her strength back at the last minute."

"Oh really?" I replied. "That's a shame, I was going to go up."

In that moment, I decided it was true. It was a great opportunity. Practice would have made me better, sure, of course, but that didn't mean I wasn't ready to go up now. I could have figured it out as I went along. That's what we'd been doing for the past few weeks, making progress every night as I snuggled up next to him in his great big bed and listened to the books he considered classics. We'd been trying for something that seemed impossible and making it up as we went. It was working for us.

"Yes," I continued with great certainty, "I would have been glad to help. If they really needed me. Or even if they didn't. If there was a costume in my size. I would have gone up. Other kids would have liked seeing a kid up there. And I'd be good at it, I bet."

My father smiled.

"I bet," he repeated.

"Maybe next time."

"Maybe next time," he repeated, pulling another sandwich from the bag and placing it on my lap.

CHAPTER THREE

Day 100

Mary was an odd, determined little person, and now she had something interesting to be determined about, she was very much absorbed, indeed.

—Francis Hodgson Burnett, *The Secret Garden*

My father closed the book with a sense of finality, despite the fact that we had a night or two worth of reading left. We'd made quite a dent in *Be a Perfect Person in Just Three Days* by Stephen Manes. The book was a short little paperback about a boy who was reading a guide to life improvement that featured some truly bizarre advice. In last night's reading, the guide prompted the boy to put a piece of broccoli on a string around his neck, and we'd howled with laughter at the idea that something so silly could actually change someone's life. Even after we'd closed it, we stayed nestled under the covers of his bed, laughing and talking about the strange guide. Tonight's chapter was just as funny, maybe even more so, but when we finished there was no laughter—well, not at first. We sat in silence for a moment or two, smiling. Then out of excitement, I did start giggling. He laughed too, but I'm not sure what he thought we were laughing about. The uncertainty made it even funnier, so we laughed until we found our way back to silence. When we sat quietly again, the air had an odd ring to it, as though it too didn't quite know what to feel. After all the anticipation and nerves, the balancing act we'd been doing, here we were. We had finished one hundred nights of reading. We had met our goal.

"What should we do to celebrate?" my father asked.

Neither of us could think of anything. We were happy, very happy, but we never did much celebrating. Years later, when my sister got into Yale, my father bought her one medium pizza from Papa John's. Which really should not have been a surprise, considering what my father eventually suggested to recognize our reading achievement.

"Let's go to Flick's in the morning," he said, sounding surprisingly excited. Well, the excitement was only surprising if you'd been to Flick's.

Flick's Cafe was best described as noncommittal. It was a small, nondescript building on the somewhat poor side of town, but by no means in the ghetto. It was rectangular and squat, with ceilings that were a bit low, but only if you really stopped to look at them. The walls were white, the floors were tiled. The tables were gray, with seats that might have gotten uncomfortable after an hour or so, but the food was always out before anyone noticed. The room smelled strongly of cigarettes, as nearly every customer lit one before or after a meal, but the air never quite got hazy. This was the place where we went to celebrate, and not because there wasn't anywhere better in Millville, New Jersey.

Well, actually, there wasn't anywhere better in Millville, to us. We had been going to Flick's for years—we couldn't even remember how the tradition started. It wasn't like my father to eat out, let alone in a sit-down establishment (or, as he describes it, the kind of place "where the butler comes around"). Somewhere along the way, though, Flick's had become the only place where my father didn't mind the "butler" and didn't even seem to mind putting down ten or fifteen dollars to help start the morning off right.

We came in and sat at our usual table by the door. We didn't need to ask for menus, because we were ordering our usual meals—pancakes for my father and cinnamon-raisin French toast for me. We kept this routine every time, as though we were making up for the noncommittal atmosphere of the place by being extremely committed ourselves. It wouldn't have seemed like much of a celebration, since it hardly differed from our norm, but again, the air had that charged feeling of accomplishment. This time the hum was most likely the air-conditioning unit beside our table, but there was still something wonderful and electrifying about the morning. Though you couldn't see the sun through the small window behind us, there were no clouds in sight and the sky was the color of an Easter egg, freshly dyed and still dripping from the experience.

I sipped a glass of iced tea, unsweetened and with lemon as always, as we waited for our food. My father, who waits until his meal comes to get a beverage, just rested his hands on the table and looked around at the other customers. He smiled a sort of goofy, far-off smile that must have attracted some attention, because the chef and owner walked over. We knew him well from our frequent visits and he usually came out to say hello, but this time he made a point of doing it before we even got our food, which was unusual.

"Jim," he said, wiping his hands on a dishtowel as he came out from the kitchen, "I've just got to ask—did you win the lottery or something? Because you haven't stopped smiling since you sat down, and you haven't even gotten my world-famous pancakes yet."

"Lovie, do you want to tell him?"

No matter how many times we visited Flick's, I still felt shy talking to Mr. Flickinger himself. He had a cheerful, childlike attitude that intimidated me more than the stuffiness of most adults. He was hard at work, but he seemed to be as happy and playful as a kitten first discovering string. He was always so genuinely happy to see us. I worried that if I couldn't match his enthusiasm first thing in the morning, he would think I was bland and dull. There is something about chipper adults that I've always found both inspiring and exhausting.

"Well, Mr. Flickinger...," I began.

"Call me Flick, you know that," he said with a wink.

"Well, Flick," I said, "we did it. We read for one hundred nights."

Just after the words had left my mouth, I realized that he probably had no idea what I was talking about. In the past fifteen or so nights, my father and I had become so driven, so goal-oriented, I had forgotten that not everyone was on a reading streak. In my mind every family was trying for a reading record. Maybe they had set the bar lower, since one hundred nights seemed impressive even once it was over, but didn't every child crawl into bed after a hot bath and snuggle up to hear a chapter or two of *Ramona the Pest* or *James and the Giant Peach*? I even thought, after reconsidering, that Flick simply didn't know because he didn't have children. Then I had to remind myself that nothing about this was normal—in the best possible way, of course—and that it might require some explanation. That was when my father jumped in.

"Well, Flick, we set a goal a while back to read for one hundred nights in a row without missing a night. Last night was the crowning gem, the one hundredth night, so we came out to celebrate in style with some of your greasy slop."

To my father, all food is "slop," or "greasy slop," and the implication that Flick's was a stylish spot for festivities did not come off without a hint of sarcasm, whether it was intended or not. Flick laughed and blushed a little, probably trying to decide if he was mildly offended or completely honored. Knowing how most people react to my father, it was probably a combination of the two that Flick hadn't realized he could feel until that very moment.

"Well this is quite the little party, then!" he said, after his face faded back to its natural color. He should have gone back to the grill a minute or two before, but nothing captured his sense of wonder more than a good story. He stood beside the table and began asking us questions.

Had it been hard? No, not particularly. We were already

in the habit of reading *almost* every night, as we always had, so it hadn't been much of an adjustment. Really, we decided, even if we hadn't been trying to keep a streak, we would have missed only six or seven of those nights. Maybe even less.

Which nights would we have missed? Well, it crossed our minds to read every night, so we never would have forgotten. But there were times when other factors would have persuaded us to take the night off, to go to bed, and leave our book untouched for just an evening. When I was sick, for example, and afraid of getting close to my father for fear of giving him the flu, I might have stayed away. Or when we stayed out particularly late (for a nine-year-old) on a couple of day trips, getting back at ten or eleven from a show or a baseball game, I think we both would have preferred slouching off to our beds and pulling the covers up to our noses. We never did, of course, because we had a goal, but the temptation was certainly there.

Did we finish every book? Well, every one so far.

Didn't the routine get boring after a while? This seemed like a silly question, and even sillier coming from a man who methodically cooked us the same meals every time we walked through his door. We were already good at routines, but The Streak was anything but. Every night was different because every story was different. Even when a book started to drag, as some did late in the second half, there was still the thrill of getting closer to our goal to make things a little more interesting. But as my father told him, and as anyone who reads regularly might agree, the only thing that has to be similar from night to night is the act of turning pages. Everything else changed as soon as we picked up a new book, plunging us deep into a new landscape with unfamiliar faces. The Streak was routine, yet it was as far from routine as anything a parent and daughter could do together.

And finally, Flick asked: what happens next? We both looked at him as though we expected him to keep talking, like he knew the answer to his own question and was just asking it as a hypothetical. We smiled at him, without saying anything, because we hadn't really talked about it yet. Mostly, we'd been talking about how we would celebrate, but we hadn't even finalized that plan until last night. We knew we would keep reading, because it was what we always did. But what came next? We shrugged and pushed our eyebrows together. We both pretended that we hadn't really been thinking about it, because we had to talk it over before we announced our official plan. My father has a competitive side that pushes him to challenge himself even in private, so it would have been impossible for him to back down from a goal once he'd told someone else. When Mr. Flickinger walked away and returned with our plates, we settled down to business.

"We need to figure out our game plan, Lovie."

I opened five butter packets as fast as I could while I considered. My father's hands always shook, and he had difficulty doing tasks that required precision, such as separating the golden foil from the plastic tub on the butter packets you get in restaurants. He liked five with his pancakes, and he liked to spread the butter while the pancakes were still piping hot, so it would melt evenly. We formed a small assembly line—I would pass him one, he would use it while I opened the next and prepared to pass it. It went without comment.

"You know," I said when his pancakes were fully buttered and I was free to enjoy my own meal, "I have been giving this a lot of consideration. Deep consideration. And after this consideration, I have decided that it is only logical for us to go for a thousand nights."

I mimed peering over my glasses and then writing a prescription. I expected my father to laugh, but his eyes got wider and wider. He stopped chewing.

"One thousand nights! What happened to two hundred, or five hundred? What's got you thinking that we should automatically multiply by ten? If we have to do that one more time, we'll go up to ten thousand nights, and I'll have to read to you in the old folks' home, shouting into your hearing aid."

"I never said anything about ten thousand nights. I said a thousand nights. Yes, that's ten times more than The Streak so far, but was it really so hard? I mean up until this point, to get where we are, was it really that tough? I feel like it wasn't. Well, it wasn't for me."

The words came out all jumbled because the idea had only occurred to me a minute or two ago. I can't remember what I was originally going to suggest, but one thousand nights wasn't it. Still, once I said it, it sounded right. One thousand nights. The one-thousand-night reading streak—that was still one less than the Arabian Nights, and just as impressive.

"Well," my father said, staring at his pancakes as though they were the ones challenging him and not me, "a lot can happen in a thousand nights. That's years, you know. You're only nine now. How old will you be then? Who knows what our lives will be like?"

Again, he looked at his pancakes instead of me. I looked over to see if they said something. Maybe the syrup had spelled out some sort of message of the future that would give my father guidance in making his decision. If it did, the syrup was on my side, because he shook his head and finally said, "But I guess it couldn't hurt to try. What the heck. One thousand nights."

I clapped my hands delightedly and waved my arms above my head. This felt like a moment I had been planning for quite some time, even if the idea had just occurred to me. Maybe it had been growing in the back of my mind for months. It couldn't have seemed more logical.

Our waitress must have interpreted my clapping and gesturing as a call for Mr. Flickinger, because when she stepped out of the kitchen he followed her back to our table.

"How's the food? Worthy of the occasion?"

I gave my father a quick, eager glance and he laughed.

"Flick, I think my daughter wants me to share some big news with you. Your restaurant has become the official sponsor of The Streak, I guess, because we set a new goal before we even finished our slop. One thousand nights. That was her idea, by the way."

He pointed at me with his knuckle as he licked syrup off of his forefinger.

I beamed up at Flick, but he looked more confused than impressed.

"Well, isn't that nice," he said with his usual enthusiasm, but not any extra.

He asked a few questions about the food, checked on our

drinks, and returned to the kitchen. He was smiling, but he didn't make the great recipient of our big news that I would have liked.

That was the first time I realized that no one, not really anyone, completely understood what we were attempting. What we were doing.

CHAPTER FOUR

Day 185

What is detestable in a pig, is more detestable in a boy.
—Charles Dickens, *Great Expectations*

A re all of our members here?" my father asked.

I pointed at myself, then at him, then nodded.

"Well then. I suppose we can call this meeting to order."

I scooched down into the hole between the vent and the window. My shirt got stuck on a nail, but my father quickly noticed and unpinned me. Tucked away from the rest of the museum, in a corner no one ever noticed, our club got under way.

"We have to sing the theme song," I said, "or else it's not an official meeting."

I cleared my throat as though I were preparing to sing opera, rubbing my neck and then moving my neck in slow, rounded movements that I'd learned from my music teacher at school.

The song was brief, but the most important part of the meeting. It had to be done right—no sloppiness or silliness.

"We're the Booooy-Haters' Club of Ameeeerica-dun!" we sang in unison.

"I think it needs to be a little louder," I said, as I noticed that some people walking by in the next room over hadn't even given us a glance. One of the number one guidelines of a club song is that it should attract attention. It's all about announcing to the world that you are here and ready to start your meeting, whether they like it or not. And if they were boys, we hoped they didn't like it at all.

"Now you're just being showy," my father said, also noticing the nearby family. But after they crossed into another exhibit, he looked to see if anyone else was coming and then nodded my cue.

"We're the Boy-Haters' Club of America!" I said, this time more of a chant.

He took his shoes off of his feet and put them on his hands like gloves, tapping out a rhythm that was in no way related to what I was singing but still seemed quite fitting. When I had finished singing or chanting the song for perhaps the tenth time and eventually tired myself out, he kept his shoes on his hands, still merrily pounding a beat to whatever song he had stuck in his head. I waited quietly for him to finish, but he continued and started bobbing his head, closing his eyes and humming. When I realized that he was actually singing a Hank Williams song, I called his attention back to the meeting. The location was sometimes distracting, but not distracting enough to excuse such behavior.

The Boy-Haters' Club of America didn't require quite the commitment that The Streak did. We were now at close to two hundred nights of reading, and we were absolutely devouring the Ramona Quimby books, reading them out of sequential order but never finding them any less entertaining. I saw some Ramona in my freckled, skinny self. As a member of the Boy-Haters' Club of America, I especially enjoyed laughing along as she chased Davy around the playground in *Ramona the Pest*. I didn't think of myself as a pest, per se, but I did my fair share of terrorizing boys when the moment called for it. The moment often did call for it, since I was a true and loyal member of the BHCA.

We met sporadically, whenever we were near the clubhouse, which was more often than you might think since it was an hour away. Our clubhouse was in the Academy of Natural Sciences in Philadelphia, on the second floor, behind an exhibit about dinosaurs. A set of carpeted steps led up to a large window with spectacular views that made it the ideal location for our meetings. There were two items on our agenda, and we had already done the first—singing the namesake song. My father wrote it, and the tune's not very specific; it is most closely related to the opening for a local news show. Because it was so short we often sang it multiple times, as we did that day, the quality of our performances going down with each repetition. Once we'd settled down from that, it was time for the second half of our club business.

"Look at that one! Geez, you can tell right away what his problem is: he's got a messy bedroom. Filthy. Dirty clothes piled everywhere, food under the bed, magazines in every corner. Disgraceful."

I hadn't been in the bedroom of any boys, but we'd read about them.

"You're not in a position to talk, Lovie. Have you seen your room in the past year or two?"

"Is this the Daughter-Haters' Club, or the Boy-Haters'? Because I am not quite a boy."

"No, not quite. Well look at this one waddling along. His problem is about as obvious as they come, all you need is one good look at him to know. He always eats with his mouth hanging open."

I squinted down at the boy, who was at this point directly below us. He did have an awfully big, pouting mouth. I wouldn't have been surprised if he didn't even have full motor control over it. Tricky.

Not everyone can tell these things about boys at first glance, especially from forty or more feet away. For many, it would take practice and some serious skill. We just happened to have both. We had been coming to our hideout for years, even back when I was in diapers, even before The Streak. It felt nice to have something secret to do right in the middle of a big public museum. It made me feel like Claudia Kincaid, hiding out in the Metropolitan Museum of Art in *From the Mixed-up Files of Mrs. Basil E. Frankweiler*. I would crawl up into my spot, stare out the window, and look for boys who were just begging for our disapproval. At first, this was difficult for me. In preschool my best friends were boys, because they shared my interest in getting our clothes as dirty as possible before the end of the day. But as I got older and boys got weirder, it became less and less of a challenge to think of things to say about them. In third grade, I now saw them for what they were: strange, foreign creatures, typically with bad breath and ill-fitting football jerseys. They had it coming, I would think. So we sat in our clubhouse and mocked them mercilessly, because there were probably boys sitting in clubhouses all over the world doing the same thing to girls and to each other. Maybe not quite the same thing, but similar. I had been meaning to ask my father something about our meetings, though. Something was suspicious.

"Dad, I've been thinking it over, and aren't you sort of a traitor for being vice president of the Boy-Haters' Club of America? I have seen your photos from elementary school and you were definitely a boy. You had the haircut and everything. And in some of the pictures you are laughing in a boy way."

"I am not trying to deny it. I was a boy. Right in there with the worst of the bunch, smelly and loud. We didn't have indoor plumbing so I always stunk. I mean I just assumed I did, I didn't notice it particularly because all boys stink around that age. I blended in quite nicely, I've got to admit."

"Yes, it sounds like you were definitely a boy. I've met boys like that, the stinky ones."

"Well, in my younger days I really wasn't so bad. I was clean and polite enough to pass for a girl. My kindergarten teacher thought my name was Jane, not James. She never figured it out, either."

"How did she never figure it out!? She thought you were a girl all along? Didn't you say anything? Didn't Grammom say something? I don't believe you. I think she was teasing you."

"No no no, I'm certain there's a jertain behind the curtain," he said, slightly misquoting Dr. Seuss's *There's a Wocket in My Pocket* to hammer his point home. "I'm certain she thought I was a girl and my name was Jane. If she were still alive today and I ran into her on the street, I think she'd call me that even now."

I looked at all six foot three of my father, his muscular frame draped in a button-up shirt and long pants. I don't think anyone could walk up to him and call him by a female name without laughing.

"Why didn't you ever correct her, if you knew she had your name *and* gender wrong?"

"Well, Lovie, don't you think Jane is a much better name than James? Hands down?"

"No! I think they are about even, but I think I'd want people to call me my name either way."

"Well, maybe someday you will change your mind. I would change my name to Jane."

"So do it. Who is stopping you? You are a grown-up and have a house and a job."

I presented this as evidence that he could do whatever he wanted without repercussions.

"That's just the problem. The papers for the house are under James. It's too late now."

I gave him a pitying look. It did make sense, though. I'd seen my father sign his name on hundreds of things, sometimes half a dozen in one day if he was paying bills. How unfortunate that people grow up using names they never liked in the first place, all because they never thought to change them. My father should have taken his opportunity to latch onto "Jane" when he had the chance. I considered calling him Jane from then on, but it wouldn't have made much sense since I'd never called him James to begin with.

"Don't worry," I said soothingly. "I talked it over with the rest of the club and being a former Jane is good enough for us. You are still a full-fledged member of the BHCA. We choose to ignore your boyhood. Though the records will indicate that you admit to being stinky, we will try to get past it."

"Thank you. Please tell the club members that I am eternally grateful for their leniency."

I looked out the window for a while. Then he turned to me and asked, sincerely, "If you ever decide you don't hate boys, will we stop having our club meetings?"

"Well, I don't really *hate* them now," I admitted. "I just hate them in spirit. So no, I don't think so. What made you think of that?"

"It could be that one day you will want to get a boy in the dreaded kiss-lock."

This was a wrestling move my father often described, where one person held the other down and forced mouth-to-face contact, usually lips to cheek; but sometimes, in a worst-case scenario, lip-to-lip contact accidentally occurred. This, he informed me, was actually poisonous and to be avoided at all costs. An accident of such proportions could be nearly fatal, if not properly treated. Sometimes it happened in the books we read and no one died, but my father was careful to remind me that those were works of fiction written for children. They left out the imminent-doom factor because it was scary.

"I know better than to do that," I said. "I am too young to risk my life for no good reason."

"There really is no good reason, you are right. It is a needless risk. When you see it in movies, they have medics standing by, waiting on the sidelines. They're highly trained professionals."

"Do other girls know this? Because no one seems to believe me at school when I bring it up. No one's even heard of the dreaded kiss-lock. They've heard of kisses, but I think that is different."

"No, not everyone knows, and you can't just go around blabbing about it, either. These are club secrets, for Pete's sake. You need to guard them with your life; anyone in a secret club knows that."

"I am sorry, I didn't realize," I said. "I thought this was public information. I understand."

I crossed my heart as though it were some sort of a club sign, though it really wasn't. We didn't have a sign or a handshake or even a high five. All the club did was sing our song and make fun of boys as they walked by. Our meetings usually lasted between two and four minutes. This one was actually on the long side, because we got sidetracked. We weren't even getting our work done. That's why I was president and he was vice president: I knew how to keep things running smoothly, and I did just that.

"Look," I said, pointing out the window again in a very businesslike manner to draw attention to the task at hand. "He sticks his gum under the desks at school. Disgusting. Never gets caught."

Just as I said this, the boy reached into his pocket and pulled out a pack of gum. He popped a piece in his mouth and carelessly threw the wrapper on the ground behind him. Predictable!

"You've really got these boys all figured out," my father said, as he helped me down from my perch. A school group was approaching the room and we couldn't risk compromising our location.

"All figured out," I said. As the group entered, a boy in the line smiled at me. I gave him a long, hard look. Then I smiled back, to avoid blowing my cover.

CHAPTER FIVE

Day 211

Memories are forever.
—Lois Lowry, *The Giver*

Franklin was named after my favorite bridge into Philadelphia. There are only two bridges, but I always had favorites of everything. He was a beta fish, brightly colored and exotic looking. Someone once told me that betas are such fighters they will attack their reflection in a mirror if they see one. Franklin never would have done this. He was a kind, loving fish.

When I read to him, which I often did, he came to the glass to listen. He would swim in place, his wide eyes looking up at me, and stay there until I put the book down and walked away. He especially liked adventure stories, which made me feel guilty because he lived in a bowl. But the bowl had a great view of our front yard, and he spent most of his time looking out at the birds and the trees. I think that made his bowl seem much bigger than it was, like living in a house made of windows.

One day as I was getting ready for school, I heard Kath and my mother whispering downstairs. My father and mother had been fighting a lot lately, and she'd even told me, in a whispered conversation a few nights before, that she was planning to move out soon. Was she telling Kath now, or did the conversation have something to do with my upcoming birthday? I stepped out into the hall and listened, but what I heard was:

"Should I wait until she gets home to tell her?"

"No, she says hello to him every morning. She will notice."

"Well what should I tell her?"

"I don't know, you're the mother. Figure something out."

I ran down the stairs and into the kitchen. Franklin's bowl was on the counter, apparently moved from the living room for better lighting. When they saw me coming they quickly jumped in front of me, but I had already seen. The bowl was empty.

"Franklin died," I stated rather than asking, already crying.

My mother looked at my sister, held her breath, and nodded.

"Egg," my sister said, using her nickname for me, "you knew this day was coming. He already lived past his life expectancy. He was pretty old, for a fish."

"But he was a happy fish," I reminded her.

"Yes," my mother said. "The world's happiest fish. You two will miss each other very much, I am sure. It is hard.

Should I ask Daddy to take care of him before you get home from school today?"

I immediately shook my head. It wasn't even an option. Franklin was my fish, not my father's. His final moments needed to be with me, and they needed to be special.

"He needs a funeral," I said. "Will you all come to his funeral? Today after school?"

"Of course we will," my mother said a little uneasily. "But don't you think that might make you a little more sad? Funerals can be very difficult, even for adults. Is this something you really want?"

"Yes, I will plan it today during school. It will be the perfect good-bye for such a good friend."

"I think you should be doing your schoolwork during school," my sister said.

"I'm in third grade," I reminded her, hoping that excused me from serious academics.

"Maybe just during lunch and recess," my mother suggested helpfully.

When I got home from school, I pulled out a folder of sketches and notes. I hadn't had enough time to organize my thoughts during lunch and recess, so I also took advantage of math, science, and social studies. On such a sad day, it's not like I could have paid much attention anyway. I had made a series of sequential drawings, and I put them in order and fanned the pages like a flip book. They didn't create any sort of moving picture, but I felt that it was a good enough preview either way. I began preparations for the event.

I'd never been to a funeral, so I went up to my father's room to thumb through the books we'd read together. Books, I was starting to discover, could be great points of reference, even if they weren't true. Some of them had a way of telling things how they were, whether they were completely true or not. They could really be helpful. I didn't remember a funeral in any of them, but maybe I'd missed it. To my surprise, none of the books my father and I had read so far even talked about death. Was he trying to protect me? I looked through the books we'd read that mentioned pets, but *It's Like This, Cat* wasn't much help. The book that focused on a girl who lived in a funeral home and would become one of my favorites from The Streak, *Each Little Bird That Sings*, would have been great help, but we wouldn't read that until years later. The Streak was still new, and there wasn't much material to work with. I decided that I didn't know much about funerals, but I sure knew a lot about parties. Were they similar? Close enough, I reasoned.

First, I made invitations. My spelling had yet to catch up with my vocabulary, but I didn't know it. To me, the letters were perfect. They read:

FRANKLIN THE FISH PAST AWAY IN HIS
SLEEP LAST NIGHT. HE WAS A DEAR FISH
AND EVERYONE WILL MISS HIM,
ESPESHULLY OUR FAMILY. PLEASE COME
TO HIS FYUNRAL TONIGHT IN ONE HOUR.
WHERE BLACK. PLEASE.

I distributed these to the family with a somber look. My father read his and said, "Lovie, in an hour I hope to be asleep. You know I need a nap after I eat. Can I just pay my respects now?"

"No," I said, "I'm sorry, but that won't work because you are the funeral speaker. You have to come out and say some nice things before we bury him, to help everyone remember him."

"Well, that is an important job. You want me to give the eulogy, then?"

"No, just some things about how great he was and how much everyone will miss him."

"All right," he said. "I will try to prepare my thoughts. It will be a privilege and an honor."

An hour later, everyone met in the kitchen, and I was disappointed to see that my father and I were the only ones appropriately dressed. My mother wore black pants with a dark blue shirt, because she didn't have any black tops. I made her go upstairs and put on lipstick to at least make her outfit a little more formal. Although she had a nice black skirt, the only black shirt my sister could find had a band's name printed across the front. I suggested that she turn it backward. The tag stuck out and scratched her neck. I told her that we all had to feel some pain when we lost a loved one.

Hors d'oeuvres were served on a silver platter that I'd constructed out of tinfoil. I knew that there should be food, but I didn't know what, so I served them the snack I usually made when I was fending for myself: wheat bread microwaved with string cheese on top, chopped up into little squares, and served with a white raisin garnish. The appetizers did not disappear as quickly as I had planned, and after ten minutes of standing around my father suggested that I leave the rest out for the birds, as a heartfelt gesture of sacrifice. It seemed right to self-lessly go without food in honor of the occasion.

We marched to the spot I had selected in the backyard, because walking was not formal enough. The location was perfect: under a great big tree, near a bush that sometimes produced flowers, in the tallest part of the grass. The leaves all fell away and then came back, so the little patch of land got sunshine in the winter and shade in the summer. Today it was a bit chilly, but bright and maybe even a little *too* cheerful. I wanted to remind the world that we were here for a funeral, not a birthday party. Had Mother Nature's father been screening the books that included death from *her*, too? The sky was supposed to be dark, and maybe a little rainy, even I knew that much. I said we were supposed to hold umbrellas, so we did, but they didn't protect us from anything aside from the occasional indignant March breeze.

First, we had a moment of silence. It went pretty well until someone started hammering a few yards over, which upset a neighbor's baby into a screaming fit, which was quickly followed by the barking of nearly every neighborhood dog. Rather than fight it, I suggested that we beautify the din by singing a song in Franklin's honor.

I had initially planned for us to sing "Both Sides Now" by Joni Mitchell, because I loved the lyrics and because my father had recently ordered a picture book version of it and informed me, to my dismay, that his students hadn't cared for it much. I knew better. But we quickly realized how confusingly repetitive the verses were. The more confused we got, the more we laughed. Well, they laughed, and I tried to keep them on track. Once it was clear that no one would actually be able to make it to the end, I resorted to my second choice song, "O Holy Night," which I chose because it was both emotional and loud. The family knew most of the lyrics this time, even though Christmas had passed a few months ago. When they got shaky, I sang even louder until the dogs started barking again. At the end of the song, I clapped. I later learned that no one ever claps at funerals, or at least the ones I've been to— not even after beautiful songs.

Franklin had been prepared for burial, at my request, in one of his fish food containers, because fish food was the thing Franklin liked best in the world. My father placed the container into the small hole I'd asked him to dig. He left the side with the ingredients facing up, but that seemed tacky. I had him turn it to reveal the photo of a bright orange fish eating tiny pellets. I asked if anyone had any comments before my father gave the eulogy. My sister began.

"It is a shame that the food pellets look pretty much the same as fish droppings. That must be confusing to them. I hope fish don't get the two mixed up."

My mother shot her a look, and my sister looked at the hole for a minute and tried again: "But Franklin never would have made that mistake, because he was such a smart fish."

I nodded approvingly and turned to my mother, who shook her head as if in great pain.

"It's hard. Well, we all loved Franklin very much. He liked to swim in circles and look at things. Sometimes when we forgot to tend his bowl, the living room smelled really bad."

She got choked up, and I went to pat her back until I realized that she was laughing. I turned and saw that my sister and father were laughing as well, behind their hands. I threw my arms up for silence.

"Enough of this disrespect! It's time for Dad to say some kind words to help us remember Franklin. Dad, have you prepared some notes that you would like to share at this time?"

My father removed an index card from his pocket. Although he tried to hold the card facing away from me, I glanced at it and saw names of students from his classes, some with checkmarks next to them. I assumed that this list somehow inspired him to really remember Franklin for all his greatness. He looked down at the card and began.

"Franklin was a good fish."

"Amen," my mother said, nodding encouragingly.

"Amen," I said. "Wait, is that it?"

"No, I was just agreeing. We can say amen to let Franklin know that we all agree."

"Amen," I repeated again. I put my hand to my heart like I was saluting the flag at school.

"Franklin was a good fish," my father continued, "And a beautiful one, too. He had bright orange fins and a very particular sense of humor. Whenever I told a joke, Franklin wouldn't laugh at all. That's because my jokes weren't funny. He was waiting for a good joke. Now, there's no more waiting."

"Amen," we all said.

"Franklin's favorite television program was *The Brady Bunch*, because he missed being a part of his big family back at the pet store. But he loved his new family, even the cats. When the cats would stare at him through the glass, he would send them good wishes. He once wished for Brian, who should have been his natural enemy, as a cat, to find a delicious bug for lunch. Well, that's exactly what happened. As you can tell, he had a big heart."

"Amen," we all said.

"Franklin had many hobbies and interests. He was especially interested in antique ladders. He would often ponder all the creative and practical uses for a good antique ladder, but he decided it wouldn't go well with the blue stones at the bottom of his bowl. That's another thing about Franklin—he had impeccable taste in art and home design."

"Amen," we all said, though I was starting to wonder where my father had gotten his information. Whatever was written on that index card, it wasn't jogging his memory too well.

"But he is probably best known for his passionate enthusiasm for competitive table hockey. When he first expressed his interest to me, in private, I told him that it was foolish. I told him that fish didn't play table hockey. Boy did he prove me wrong. No sooner had I told him he couldn't do it than he became the local champion in the fish league. He fought long and hard to have table hockey included in the Olympics, and the committees are, at this very moment, considering his request. He made great progress for both the sport and the fish who love it."

"Amen," my sister and mother said, but they were smiling.

"Hey wait a minute, I don't remember any of this stuff."

"And," my father continued, "who can forget his masterful skill at tailoring outfits for special occasions and events. Why, it seems like just yesterday that I came down the stairs and saw—"

I looked up to see that my mother and sister were doubled over, tears streaming down their faces. But they were not mourning. They were laughing.

"None of that ever happened, and this is a serious time!" I shouted.

They quieted down for a moment, and I stopped my father before he could continue his speech.

"I have an announcement. For the rest of my life, I am giving up fish and sea creatures of all kinds. In honor of my good friend, Franklin the fish. Thank you all for coming. Please leave before you disrespect the grave of such a beautiful creature."

I marched back inside to set the example, lifting my legs high and waving my stiff arms.

"When do you think you'll go back to eating fish?" my sister asked, as she marched behind me.

"If you were listening instead of clowning around, you might have heard that I said I will not be eating fish or sea creatures of any kind for the rest of my life."

"Oh, yes, for the rest of your life. I forgot," she said.

Franklin, if you are listening: I am twenty-two years old. I haven't had fish or sea creatures of any kind since the day you died. Please excuse my family's disrespect.

PS: I never knew how much you liked table hockey.

CHAPTER SIX

Day 440

But Mama is far ahead, and she doesn't look back. She is somewhere else.

—Patricia MacLachlan, *Journey*

I always hated Thanksgiving. With a stomach the size of a pincushion, I never got into the idea of a holiday devoted to eating. I liked to eat, of course, but I also liked stopping when I was full. And I didn't like turkey, or stuffing if it had been in the turkey (name one other food that people *prefer* to eat out of a carcass), or gravy, or cranberry sauce. Plus, we always floated from aunt to aunt while everyone else I knew went to the same house every year. Recently, we'd started eating at home, and I still didn't like the food. So I never had high expectations for the holiday, and this cloudy November afternoon was no exception.

In fact, the only thing worth devoting any enthusiasm to

was the cloudy sky. Three years ago, it snowed on Thanks-giving. It didn't seem entirely impossible this year, if the weather held. I loved snow. I had the best sled in town, hands down—a smooth surfboard that just so happened to be the fastest thing on the hill every year. I also had a great collection of jackets and scarves, which looked particularly good with little flecks of white on them. I had already picked out the perfect combination—a bright blue jacket with a unicorn scarf—and hid them under my bed. Leaving them out in the open would be jinxing it. But I felt pretty certain. Today, it would snow.

My father was outside raking, since taking any sort of day off made him antsy, and I was dutifully fulfilling my role in the process. As soon as he brought the leaves to the pile at the front of the yard, I would jump in them and let him know that it was a good amount, but more would be even better. This provided inspiration for him to keep raking. I told him this every time he asked me to get out of the pile so he could get some work done.

I was standing in this pile when I noticed my mother carrying some boxes to her car. I looked at her for a while without moving, watching her take several trips, but I was unable to figure out what she was doing. I felt like Encyclopedia Brown and enjoyed piecing together the clues, just like him, to try to come to some sort of a conclusion about this mystery. My father said that though he loved the Encyclopedia Brown books as much as I did, they gave kids unrealistic expectations—some of the things the boy wonder knew were things even my father, a teacher and voracious reader with a college education, had never heard. I knew mystery solving was a challenge, but unlike Encyclopedia I didn't have a nemesis like Bugs Meany breathing down my neck. I needed to close my eyes and think deeply, the way he did at the end of every story, but I couldn't watch what my mom was doing with my eyes closed. I remembered that the eye-closing part came only after Encyclopedia had lots of information, so I observed.

At first, I assumed my mother's actions had something to do with the meal. Even though our dinner was small (my sister was an exchange student in Germany that year, so it was just the three of us), I imagined that it would take a few hours to get everything ready. I felt bad for not offering to help. I liked leaves better than the kitchen, but she seemed really busy, and whatever she was doing looked exhausting. I still couldn't figure out what the boxes had to do with dinner, though. Had she borrowed pots and pans from someone? Probably. Neither of my parents cooked often. I thought my dad might offer to help her carry the boxes, but he'd moved to the backyard and apparently didn't notice her. I decided that Encyclopedia must have had more clues than this. Finally I went inside.

The first thing I noticed when I came up to my parents' bedroom was that my mother's perfumes and jewelry, usually jumbled together on a white tray on the bureau, were gone. All that was left was a green earring, which I picked up. These were the sort of earrings that my mother wore to her job as a high school English teacher. I thought everything she wore to work smelled like her school, a comforting smell of coffee and perfume. I put the earring to my nose and smelled nothing. I looked for the rest of her jewelry. My initial reaction was that it had been stolen, until I noticed my mother crouched beside the bed, cramming her books into boxes.

"What are you doing?" I asked, suddenly noticing how empty the room was.

She was clearly annoyed.

"I'm moving out," she said. "We talked about this. We've been talking about this for months."

"Yes, but today?"

"Right now."

I didn't know what to say. I couldn't deny it—I knew she was going to move out someday, she had brought it up before and even asked for my advice picking out an apartment. But the idea seemed distant, almost hypothetical: she was going to move out in the same way that I was going to drive a car. Someday. Eventually.

"Well, on Thanksgiving?" I asked.

In my mind, I remember her turning to me and saying, "You don't even like Thanksgiving." But actually, I don't think she knew that about me. It wasn't something I started verbalizing until later. It seemed unpatriotic and I felt guilty.

She asked me to help load some of her things into boxes, and I did, because I didn't know what else to do. She had a lot of things. Even after she moved out, that is something I always remembered about my mother—all the things she had. Boxes and bags and things absolutely everywhere—so many things that she hadn't even had time to unwrap some of them after buying them. There was a lot more than could fit into her car, but she said she would come back for more tomorrow.

That was a little comforting. If some of her stuff was here, she might decide to stay. I put the green earring that didn't smell like her or like anything into my pocket. Now she *had* to come back for something, no matter how much she managed to cram into this trip.

We carried the boxes to the car, which struck me as a lot roomier than I remembered. We made trip after trip before I realized that she hadn't told me where she would be staying.

"Remember the apartments we looked at five minutes away, by the high school?"

"The one with the ducks?"

"No, the one with the pool."

I must have perked up at this, because she smiled a little.

"I'm not really leaving. I'll be right down the road, and there will be a pool, and you can have your own bedroom."

"Do I have a bed?"

"Of course you don't have a bed yet. *I* don't have a bed yet. You'll get one."

Even then, for some reason I found this too hard to believe. Where would she get the money for one bed, let alone two? In my mind, my mother did all of the spending and my father did all of the earning. It didn't matter that her job as a Catholic schoolteacher came with a fairly reasonable salary. We were in debt. I didn't know how much debt, but judging by how often the phone rang and creepy, insistent automated voices spoke at the other end, we probably owed someone a lot of money. And I never knew my father to buy anything at all, so as far as I could tell, my mother was in trouble, and she would be in trouble no matter where she went.

It was as I was taping one of the boxes shut that I noticed she was not crying. My mother cried over everything, from Christmas cards to friendly teasing, so this shocked me. I could not take my eyes off of hers. They were small and brown and puffy—perhaps she had been crying earlier?—but they were dry. Noticing this had a stronger impact on me than her tears ever had. Those had become commonplace, but these new eyes, dry in spite of what I knew to be a monumental change for both of us, were alarming. Like the boxes I'd seen her carrying to the car, these eyes took me a few minutes to interpret. But when I finally came to a conclusion, it was that she was really leaving and was happy to go.

This made sense. My mother and father rarely spoke to each other; more often, they yelled, and whatever speaking was done was never constructive. A discussion about whether or not to turn on the air conditioner could easily result in two or more hours of intense battle, my mother crying for every minute of it and my father methodically making his points until he realized she wasn't the most captive audience. Considering myself an expert at debate, I always took a side, but defended both parents almost equally, on different days.

I had even been able to defend, on my more skillful days, my mother's phone calls with men. She was sad and lonely. The men would call while my father was not around, which struck me as strangely polite, and she would talk to them in hushed tones on the basement steps. I don't know if she ever met with the men in person, but she was not flaunting these men in his face; her phone calls and e-mails—and visits, if they happened—were barely more than a distraction in most cases.

I wondered, as we struggled to close the trunk over our final load, whether any of these men would be at the apartment.

"Of course he'll come visit," she said of her current boyfriend. "But he won't live there."

Which was just as well, because I didn't want anyone taking my room, bed or no bed.

As my mother was backing out of the driveway, I couldn't tell if she was finally crying or squinting from the sun, which was now peeking out curiously at us from behind the clouds. My hopes for snow were dashed, and I went inside to watch a cartoon marathon, though I hated cartoons.

Half an hour later, my father came in.

"You know your mother did not come out *once* to offer me a glass of water?" he called to me from the door. He took his gloves off as he walked to the oven and opened the door. Seeing nothing inside, he asked, "What's the deal with the turkey?"

"Huh?" I'd been trying to braid my hair for months and I was finally making progress on a nice thin one across my forehead.

"What's the deal with the turkey?" he repeated. "Don't those things take hours?"

He looked at the clock. It was dinnertime, or close enough.

His confusion didn't register with me.

"Well, are you going to make it?" I asked, not looking up from my braid.

"Why would I make it? I just spent six hours raking, and I'm not even done in the backyard. Can't your mother do anything around here? Where is she?"

He called up the stairs, "It's five o'clock in the library!"

As you might imagine, anyplace where my father was, especially our house filled with books, was "the library." The phrasing didn't surprise me, but the action did. Until I realized.

"Oh," I said, suddenly feeling very guilty without knowing why. "Mom left."

"Mom left? Where did she go? When's she putting the turkey in?"

"No, *left* left. Moved out."

My father didn't seem to hear me but wordlessly moved up the stairs and to his bedroom. I heard him walking around up there, opening the closet and an occasional drawer. The creaks of the house were familiar, and I knew when I heard him pause in front of the window that he was looking for her car. After some time, he came back downstairs. I turned off the television.

"Do we still have the turkey?"

I checked the fridge, then the freezer, and handed it to him.

"Do you know how to make this thing?"

I shrugged. I didn't want to say no, since it seemed like something interesting to try. Also, I'd seen other people do it. Turn on the oven, put in the turkey, cut it up. Simple. But my father didn't seem to think so, because he said, "We don't know what to do with this thing."

I shook my head. If he thought we didn't, we probably didn't.

He put the carcass back in the freezer and pulled out the box next to it.

"Meatballs," he said flatly.

"*Swedish* meatballs," I corrected him. These were on the list of things I hated—a list that can be very long at ten years old but still felt short in length to the list of things I absolutely loved. Like sledding, and wearing scarves.

"Do you think it will snow?" I asked.

"None of the stations predicted that," he said as he wrapped the meatballs in a paper towel and pressed 3:33 on the microwave. I was pretty sure that the box hadn't said to do that, but he'd already torn it up.

I poured myself some milk and sat at the table. He put a few meatballs on a paper plate and I chewed them slowly, using my hands to eat them for no particular reason. The brown lumps were a bit cold in the center. I noticed that my father wasn't saying anything. I wondered if that meant I should.

"I wasn't really looking forward to the turkey," I said finally.

"Neither was I," he said. "I only really like the mashed potatoes, anyhow."

He turned on the news and we ate in silence.

CHAPTER SEVEN

Day 529

The longer she read the more wonderful and more real the pictures became.

—C. S. Lewis, *The Voyage of the Dawn Treader*

If your father is an eccentric and excitable children's librarian like mine, or even if he's not, you may very well know about the joy of book fairs. Even if your father is a dancer or a plumber or a professional teapot designer, you have probably still experienced a book fair. You need only to have a kid or be a kid to remember the thrill of walking into the library (or gym or cafeteria) and seeing those big silver cases, all lined up in a row, waiting patiently for someone like you to wander over and pick out something nice. And if you've ever been there the day before the fair starts, when the cases are still locked shut, you know the anticipation, the agony, of staring at those boxes and wondering what you're in for this year. If there was a new kid in your class, someone who had never had the happiness of attending a book fair before, it was your duty and your pleasure to fill him or her in on the process. As uncomplicated as it may be, you, or at least I, had to make sure that no one was left out of the fun.

So it was only natural that when my father asked for my help at his book fair one year, I went all out. The book fair lasted several days, including his back-to-school night, which meant that I could attend even though I was in school during his school day. I began where any logical fourth grader knows to begin: plopped down on the floor in front of a pile of white papers and a sixty-four-color box of crayons.

I like to think that I am very handy with a cache of crayons. Although I've never quite figured out how to use the in-box sharpener (contrary to its name, it rounds the crayons rather than sharpening them), I make do. Every good fair needs signs, especially a book fair. So I set to work designing signs with characters from some of my favorite books of The Streak: Alice, Dorothy, Sherlock Holmes...anyone who was anyone was going to make an appearance. Then I labeled each poster with the title and the author, so that interested readers could find the books and take them home. That is the best part, after all; even better than holding, touching, smelling, and hugging new books is taking them home and reading them in your own bed, under your own covers, with your own lamp shining beside you until someone yells for you to turn it off and get some sleep.

I put lots of time and effort into those posters, perhaps a full half hour for twenty of them, and when they were done,

I was eager to display them as part of my sales pitch. This year, thanks to me, my father would sell more books than ever before. More kids would get yelled at for having the light on in the middle of the night, and more parents would be secretly pleased when they peeked in and saw the beam of a flashlight shining resiliently through the covers. This was my goal: the best book fair ever. With my help and guidance, it was beyond possible. It was probable. It was certain, actually.

"Why does this mummy look like he is scared and looking for a bathroom?" my father asked, pointing to an R. L. Stein character from a book I'd read on my own. He wanted to examine my work and fully understand it before letting me hang it on his library walls. I respected his desire for quality, but I didn't appreciate the attack on my work.

"Well, you haven't read that book, have you? That is exactly what it is about."

"There is a Goosebumps book about a terrified mummy who can't find the bathroom?"

"Yes, it is less popular than the others, as you might guess, but it has its place with real fans."

"I can only imagine," he said, flipping through the rest of my work more quickly.

"Well," he said when he reached the end, "I think these posters are definitely about books."

My father will not lie, so he tries to say the best possible thing that is also the truth. He doesn't realize that this is often worse than just saying what he thinks as nicely as possible. I was used to it and accepted his comments with a shrug, as I did now, but he wasn't always so lucky. Once, a friend of his made him cookies for his birthday and he accidentally started an argument by saying, when she asked what he thought of them, "I can honestly say that every one of those cookies has chocolate chips in it."

But because he hadn't come right out and said he thought my posters were sloppy, I happily gathered them up in my arms, grabbed a roll of masking tape, and headed for the car. On the way to the school we also stopped to pick up a friend of mine. Brittany was usually ready for whatever idea I had at the moment, and helping me host a book fair didn't even seem particularly odd to her. She didn't ask what her job would be or when we would be going home. She was a good friend to have.

When we arrived, we taped the posters just about everywhere in the library, to be sure we got the point across. Yes, fitting with tradition, we hung some on the walls. But also, for the sake of surprise, we hung some on the desks. And taped a few to the carpet. And just in case a smaller kid decided to go crawling around on his hands and knees under the conference table covered in discounted paperbacks, there was a poster hanging upside down in there, just for him. We were there to divide and conquer.

Parents started to trickle in, some with kids and some alone. In no time the room was buzzing with potential customers. Now was a great opportunity to try out my sales pitch: I stood on a chair, cupped my hands like a megaphone, and began making announcements. Parents must be immune to the voices of obnoxious children, because they were able to tune out such messages as:

"BOOKS ARE COLLECTORS' ITEMS, ESPE-
CIALLY IF YOU COLLECT BOOKS."

And the cryptic, mock-prophetic,

"NOW IS THE TIME TO BUY. NOT LATER.
NOW! BEFORE IT'S TOO LATE."

And my crowning glory, one that I spent over a week
mulling over and reworking,

"ATTENTION PARENTS: EVERY BOOK PUR-
CHASED TONIGHT AUTOMATICALLY COMES
WITH THE LOVE AND APPRECIATION OF
ONE IMPORTANT CHILD—YOURS."

The last was loosely based on an ad about feeding homeless
children, but it did make people pause and look up at me curiously, wondering who I was and why this nice librarian was
letting me stand on his chairs and yell things at his customers.
Sometimes a good sale calls for some mystery.

A few hours into the sale my voice was getting hoarse and
my signs were falling down. I stopped by my father's makeshift cash register for some shop talk. Sales were good, he
admitted, but not as good as I'd predicted.

"If this is really going to be the best book fair ever," he
said, "you'd better have another trick up your sleeve. So far it
is maybe the second or third best. You don't want people to
think you were slacking on the job, do you?"

I decided to go to the school's office and make an announcement over the intercom, since the events of the evening were officially over and I would not be disturbing anyone any more than usual. Brittany followed, making suggestions over my shoulder and occasionally taking the mic herself when my thirty-second promos were starting to lose steam. Hearing your voice amplified is secretly a treat for almost anyone, but especially kids. We made several trips to the office that night.

"I think the customers are really starting to get the message," my father said at one point.

"Do you mean that I should stop? Or should I make them shorter? I think they're just right."

"Maybe your next announcement should be your last, to give people time to fully process the advice. Then they can really reflect on your words and meditate on the book fair experience."

Before he could finish letting me down gently, though, he was interrupted by a boy who had been trying for the last half hour to get a second free book out of a buy-one-get-one-free sale.

"But I'm not me this time. I'm my brother," I heard the boy explaining as I closed the door.

Brittany and I wandered back into the office and rehearsed a script before taking to the airwaves. The last broadcast had included singing, but this one focused on a bit of "candid" discussion about my father's library skills. Somewhere along the way I had changed the project from marketing the book sale, to marketing the library, to marketing my father as a librarian. Then, even if book sales were low, people would think back to the fair and remember what a great man my father was.

"Wow," Brittany said into the microphone when we were ready, "this service is great!"

"Yes," I said, trying to disguise my voice so people wouldn't dismiss my compliments as biased, "Mr. Brozina is a great librarian. He is ready and waiting to help you pick out a book at the book fair!"

"But what if I don't know what to chase?" Whispering and rattling of papers. "I mean choose!"

"There are helpful posters all over the library, and Mr. Brozina has even more good ideas."

"Wow, I should get going. I don't want to miss the fair. Do I have time? Where is it again?"

"The library is on the second floor at the top of the stairs. You have until nine. Run, run!"

I turned off the microphone and pointed at the door. During our announcement, an office worker had squeezed past us, turned off the lights, closed the door, put a key in the lock, and done *something*. I wasn't sure what. I assumed she'd locked the door, but I also assumed it didn't lock from the inside. It couldn't have, or else she wouldn't have locked it—she had made eye contact with us and smiled. She knew we were in here. Actually, there was no doubt the whole school knew we were in here. But as soon as I put down the microphone I ran to the door and checked the knob, just to be sure.

"Locked!" I shouted. Brittany came over and pulled on it herself. We wrenched the handle, leaning our body weight on the door as we pushed and hanging without our feet touching the ground when we pulled. I imagine we looked like Atlas trying to hold up the world instead of open a door.

When I finally realized that we weren't going to make any progress on the door itself, we tried screaming through the crack under it. The evening events were coming to a close, and no one was anywhere nearby. So we started combing the room for possible escape routes. We were on the second story—the windows were out of the question. And we couldn't see a door on the other side of the room. It quickly became apparent that whoever built this office had never been locked in it.

"Maybe this was part of the Underground Railroad," I suggested, thinking back to my social studies class. "And there is a door, but we can't see it because they had to hide it. Maybe it's a secret little door, hidden behind the fax machine."

Ten minutes later, sweaty and exhausted from moving the cumbersome piece of equipment, I decided that a fax machine was an absolutely worthless piece of machinery, especially if it wasn't even being used to cover up a secret door. I announced that we should look around for a wardrobe, in case the Wood School office had anything in common with the world of *The Lion, the Witch and the Wardrobe*, a book my father and I had just recently started and one that I found particularly thrilling. Why should Susan—or Alice or Dorothy, for that matter—be any different from me? If they could find portals to other worlds in their everyday lives, so could I. In fact, it seemed almost certain that I would someday. I checked my closets often, but they didn't seem nearly mysterious enough. This office would perhaps prove more inspiring. It was certainly hiding *something*.

"Would a wardrobe look like a closet filled with paper and staplers and stuff?" Brittany asked.

"No, it would be more like a magical portal to another world. There would be fur coats."

"No, nothing like that in here," she said, reaching her hand into a closet to feel around, "But I did find a barrel of flavored Tootsie Rolls. Just the lemon ones; someone ate everything else."

"Count them," I said, "We are going to need rations. I need at least seven lemon Tootsie Rolls to last until morning. If they were orange, I could live on four. But lemon doesn't stick to your bones."

"Last until morning? It's not even nine o'clock yet! Why wouldn't we get out of here until morning?"

"If you've got a way out I'm happy to hear it," I said, folding my legs pretzel style and carefully unwrapping my first lemon Tootsie Roll. I ate it slowly, savoring each bite, sure it would be my last.

"Why don't we just make an announcement?" she said, walking back to the microphone.

"Huh?"

"Just make an announcement that we're locked in here. We already know how this thing works."

"Why didn't you say this before! I was preparing to face my death!"

"I noticed," she said. She handed me the microphone and switched it on.

I thought for a moment. I wanted to be sure that whatever I said didn't create too much panic.

"ATTENTION, THERE ARE TWO SMALL CHIL-DREN TRAPPED IN THE R.D. WOOD SCHOOL

OFFICE. PLEASE SEND SOMEONE TO SAVE THEM IMMEDIATELY."

I stepped away from the microphone and huddled close to Brittany for warmth until she reminded me that it was actually unpleasantly hot in the office. I ate another Tootsie Roll.

Finally, my father appeared through the office window, laughing and talking to a janitor.

"*Dad!*" I yelled through the door. "We're in here! We're in here! Open the door!"

"What do you think I came down to the office for? To see what I thought of the wallpaper?"

He opened the door and I ran to him.

"You saved us!" I yelled, jumping up and down and grabbing his hand.

He laughed and started walking back to the library, and we ran to catch up.

"Someday, I will tell my children this story," I continued. "Of how I risked my life for the book fair. And it will make them think about the importance of books, and how wonderful they are."

"No, it will make them realize their mother was a complete loon," he corrected me.

Then he opened the cash box and took out a sheet of paper with the total sales: the highest in ten years.

CHAPTER EIGHT

Day 646

*"Well, I am pretty," replied Charlotte. "There's no denying
that. Almost all spiders are rather nice-looking. I'm not as
flashy as some, but I'll do."*

—E. B. White, *Charlotte's Web*

I don't think they're actually spiders," my dad said, as we
turned the porch light on for a better look.

"What else would they be? Long legs, little body...he
looks like one."

"Well it's probably a she. And maybe it's an arachnid?"

"Aren't arachnids spiders?"

I was eleven and as full of answers as I was questions.

"We could look it up in the encyclopedia," he said,
"Though I'm not sure what they're really called. I kind of
doubt they would be listed under 'daddy long-legger.'"

The little creature crawled slowly up the supports of our porch,
tapping her legs like long fingernails, making her look impatient.

"I like her colors," I said, reaching out to stroke one of the legs.

"Careful, you'll hurt her!" He didn't stop my hand, but I pulled it back.

"I wouldn't hurt you," I whispered.

I wasn't sure where her eyes were, but I imagined that they were looking at me with trust. Spiders, or in this case, spider-like things, should have known to trust us. My father and I were the protectors, advocates, and general fans of any and all spiders. The absolute best spot for spiders was our front porch. The light attracted other bugs, who usually looked big and clumsy to me. The spiders would catch them and wrap them up tightly, as though they were going to exchange them as gifts. I think that spiders are always afraid that someone is going to invite them to a birthday party at the last minute, and they want to be ready. The little white dots in the corner of a web are always so tidy, and kind of lovely. Then a horrible thought occurred to me.

"Dad, you don't think Bertha will eat her, do you? I mean if this thing's not a spider, is she in danger?"

Bertha was the crowning glory of our porch. An absolutely gorgeous, thick, dark brown beauty resembling a miniature tarantula, she was the topic of many excited conversations. I named her the first night I saw her, because if you're going to have a guest, you might as well know what to call her. Bertha must have felt quite welcome. She had already been on our porch for over a month, weaving her web by moonlight every evening, waiting for "customers," as my father called them. No matter how early we got up, though, the web was gone every morning. We couldn't imagine that she'd actually taken it down—they were always intricate and beautifully, painstakingly symmetrical. But they also looked too sturdy to blow away in the breeze, so we couldn't explain where they went. They were as mysterious as she was. Right now, however, the web was up, Bertha was seated near the center of it, and no customers had come yet. I was worried for our new friend, the not-spider.

"No," my father said, "if she's quick on her feet she's safe from Bertha. And look how lively she is! She can take care of herself, I'm sure."

His voice was filled with wonder as he looked from Bertha to the newcomer, and I knew he was about to begin his almost nightly lecture on their beauty. I always wanted to hear it, so I prompted him.

"Dad, why do you like spiders so much?"

He sighed a contented sigh and stared dreamily at the complex web.

"Well, Lovie, it's like we always say. I like that they're active. They don't just sit on a plant and sunbathe. They go out and find something to do, like make this web, and then they catch things, and then they put them in storage. I like the way they walk, the way they lift their legs like they're walking through puddles gracefully. And I like that they're underrated. Everyone thinks they're harmful but they're really quite beneficial."

"What if you woke up and there was a spider on you?"

"At least you know there aren't any other bugs on you!"

"What if it was a big one?"

"The bigger the better!"

"The bigger the better," I repeated, noticing movement in Bertha's web. I jumped to my feet, thinking she'd caught something, but when I saw that the web was empty, I realized: "That noise in the distance must be thunder!"

"Geezlepeezle!" my father exclaimed. "I almost forgot, there's a huge storm predicted tonight. Good thing we finished our reading in time to see it!"

Of course, he hadn't forgotten. That's why we'd come straight to the porch after we finished a chapter of *It's Like This, Cat*. Partly to check on Bertha, of course, but also to observe another beloved sight: the coming of a summer storm.

We turned off the porch light (I apologized to Bertha in case it would hurt her business) to get the full effect of the lightning and ate pineapple juice pops while we waited, getting more excited as the time between the lightning and thunder got smaller. In school we'd learned that for every "Mississippi" you could say between seeing the lightning and hearing the thunder, the storm was a certain number of miles away. I forgot how many miles it was exactly, but right now the storm was six Mississippis away, which seemed impressive. I told my father this with excitement. He smiled.

"Do you remember being scared of storms?" he asked.

"No," I said dismissively, "I was never afraid of storms. You must be thinking of Spider."

Appropriately enough, this was also our nickname for my sister, because of her long, thin legs. Partly because she was seven-and-a-half years my elder and partly because she was on the tall side, her legs always seemed to me twice the size of my entire body. There were few things I loved as thoroughly as spiders, but my older, cooler sister was one of them. The comparison was the highest compliment to both of course.

"No no, it was you," he said emphatically. "When you were two years old, maybe even as late as three, you were terrified of thunderstorms. Your mother started that in you. The thunder would get to rumbling off in the distance, and she would call you inside immediately, and make it all out as the most horrible thing to ever happen on Hazel Boulevard."

I still didn't believe him.

"If I was scared of them then, why aren't I scared of them now?" I asked suspiciously.

"You think I was going to let you be afraid of something as beautiful as a thunderstorm? Like fun! As soon as I realized what your mother was up to, I brought you out on the porch, right in the heart of the storm, and every time we would see a lightning bolt I would yell, 'That's a good one!'"

"What did I do?"

"What do you do now? After a few minutes, you started yelling, 'That's a good one!' and hopping up and down like a frog, 'That's a good one! That's a good one!' You would hop and hop and hop, cheering with all the life in you and shaking your little fists, even when the lightning was right overhead! Sometimes I thought the house was going to crack open. But as long as we were under the roof of the porch and close to the house, I figured we were reasonably safe. As safe as anywhere, I'd imagine."

The storm was getting closer and the windows were starting to shake beautifully, humming with the excitement and anticipation.

"So the only reason I like storms is because you convinced me to?"

"You liked storms because they were fun! The sky lights up. You can see the whole street. Also they're loud. And maybe a little dangerous."

He was also describing the current scene, as the sky broke open with a crack and a torrential downpour began. My first instinct was to check to see if Bertha was safe, but she was a smart girl and had already headed for her rain spot, hidden behind the gutter. You had to know where to look, because only one brown leg was sticking out, almost flirtatiously, against the white paint. The newcomer had moved to the window, and I couldn't tell if she was looking in or looking out. With all those eyes, it was probably both.

"I was never afraid of spiders, was I?" I had to ask, even though I knew that an affirmative answer would be the ultimate shame.

"I don't recall that you were," he laughed. "But I took preventative measures."

I remembered *Charlotte's Web,* and how it had been one of the first books we ever read together. Charlotte was my favorite character in the book, before Wilbur or even Templeton. She used her webs to spell out words just as I was learning to spell them myself, and I knew how proud of herself she must be. All words look beautiful in your own handwriting, so they would have looked even prettier on a web. Maybe Bertha was writing words, too, but since there was no pig in need of saving she needn't bother to write them in English. They were in spider language, with tight capital letters that people couldn't read. Charlotte would have known what they said—she was great with languages. English, spider language, pig or rat or goose language, she could do it all and still have time to make something beautiful. But that didn't make me respect Bertha any less, because she was real, and she was ours.

"I would have liked spiders on my own," I insisted.

I just would have, because of their colors and their eyes and their gift-wrapping technique and their dazzling webs. And their legs, like my sister's.

"You didn't even name Bertha," I pointed out. "That was me."

"Yes, you probably always liked spiders," he agreed.

I still felt a little cheated, since he was trying to take all the credit. But he had gotten me thinking, and I was feeling something else, too.

Really, secretly, I was a little proud. Proud to love storms and spiders, things most of my friends hated. Proud to be fearlessly out on the porch watching the wind whip the trees and waiting for lightning to strike. Even if he *had* coaxed me out of a fear years ago, was that so bad? Anything was better than hiding in my bed, pulling the covers up over my head and waiting for the storm to pass like I'd seen girls do at sleepovers. And now, my excitement was all my own, bubbling over in me without his help.

When lightning finally struck in plain sight, lighting our faces like a flash photograph, we both rose to our feet at the same time. But the line was mine to say, and I relished it.

"THAT'S A GOOD ONE!" I yelled, jumping up and down, shaking my fists in triumph.

CHAPTER NINE

Day 758

Everybody cried, because death is hard. Death is sad. But death is part of life. When someone you know dies, it's your job to keep on living.

—Deborah Wiles, *Each Little Bird That Sings*

I never really thought of my grandfather as my father's father. I couldn't picture him as a young person, meeting my grandmother and picking out a ring. I knew that he was something in the war, but I don't think anyone knew for sure exactly what he did. At some point his children were born, and he raised them, and then he became Poppop. I didn't know much about Charles Brozina, but as Poppop, he was at least familiar.

Poppop kept a garden behind the house, where he raised the usual Jersey things, like squash and strawberries and tomatoes bigger than both my fists together. He'd go out to work in the garden for hours every day, sweating though his striped gray overalls that might have been blue once. It was only a few months before he died when I realized that he was a retired road worker with a hobbyist's garden and not the full-time farmer I'd always assumed he was. He never mentioned his old line of work to me, but he always sent me home with a crinkly plastic bag of produce, so for years I wanted to be a farmer. He smelled of soil and Ivory soap, which struck me as the perfect combination.

I don't remember much from his funeral other than that the smell was gone, the way my mother's smell went away the day she moved out. The room with my grandfather's casket smelled like flowers and perfume and wood polish, but there was no hint of dirt or soap. There were little cardboard prayer cards, one of which I folded into tiny squares until my sister told me I might want it someday. The rest of the day has faded with time. What I remember from that week happened the night before.

Before the viewing, my father and his siblings were called to the funeral parlor to make sure their father looked just as they wanted him to for the next morning. When my dad got home from the event and came up for our reading, he looked a little shaken. Since the event had seemed mostly a formality (he had seen the body before), I was a bit taken aback to see him affected by it. We hadn't talked about the passing of his father, so when I asked him what was wrong, I was expecting the kind of conversation I knew from sitcoms. Poppop was gone. He wasn't coming back, but he was in a better place. I would feel better in time, but never forget him. I certainly had not expected my father to talk about his feelings, especially with me. A little over a decade of life experience seemed hardly enough to qualify me for the position of compassionate listener. But as I sat beside him on his bed, nodding my head and asking questions at the right moments, that was what I tried to be. He began without much prompting, which made me even more certain that he was sharing his burden rather than trying to explain death.

"We were all standing around the casket," he explained in a calm but surprisingly soft voice, "and the room was crowded, since there was Grandmom and the four of us. Everyone else managed to get spots right up close, looking at him, but there was no room for me. I tried to squeeze in but when I didn't fit I had to go down and stand by his feet."

I nodded and used a phrase I had recently learned at school: "And how did that make you feel?"

"Well, at first I was pretty annoyed. I wanted to see him as much as the rest of them, and even as tall as I am it's not like I could see over my brothers. So I was stuck at the feet and I wasn't too happy about it. What kind of feedback could I give the funeral director about the feet? That the shoes needed some shining?"

"Did they?"

He ignored this question, and I made a mental note that my questions only worked if they got him talking about the things he already wanted to talk about. I tried to be the best possible listener, not even biting my nails. Well, biting them a little, but only to help me concentrate.

"I stood there sort of brooding, waiting for my chance to move up to the head of the casket, but then I actually started looking at his feet. When I looked at them, they made me think."

"What did they make you think of?"

It was obvious that he was going to tell me anyway, but I wanted him to know that I was really listening, and that I wasn't scared to hear his real thoughts on death, even if parents usually hid them.

"They made me think of the times when I was a kid." The strain in his voice told me this was the part that had him shaken. "And he would pay me a nickel to rub them. When he got home from work and his feet were sore, he would pay me a nickel to rub his feet, and I'd use the nickel to buy baseball cards. There were four of us, you know, but I don't know if he asked anyone else to rub his feet. That was our thing, as far as I can remember."

He let out a sigh after saying it, like it hurt a little more to get it out than it did to keep it in. I warned myself never to make him repeat it, no matter how old I got. It felt like a secret.

"Didn't you have other things? Things that you shared, like The Streak?"

"Nothing like The Streak. We both liked baseball, but my brother liked baseball."

He thought for a moment, and again I knew that this was the right question. I looked at myself in the mirror across from his bed, checking to see if I suddenly looked a little taller or more adult. I thought I did. Maybe a little. My father looked as big as ever, but his size was all huddled up in a lump, curled up on itself like he was bracing for a storm.

"Well, boxing was our thing. We would watch the fights together on Fairton Road when I still lived there, and when I moved he would come here to watch them. Sometimes I took him to see them in person. We saw some pretty good fights."

"So it's not like all you ever did, just the two of you, was rub his feet."

"There was more than that, but not much more than that. It's hard with four. How do you ever spend time with one? What are the other three doing? When you finally do spend time alone together, it's not until you're both adults. And then I can't say it's quite the same. Not the same as getting to know them when they're still trying to figure things out about the world."

"But you're still trying to figure things out about the world even now, aren't you?"

"That's very true. Are you?"

"Yes, there's lots I want to figure out. I'm sure Spider has lots to figure out, too," I said, pointing to a photo of my sister on his nightstand.

"Two is a lot easier than four."

"But you still had time to get to know Poppop, I mean your dad. Right? Plenty of time."

He shook his head in a way that could have been a dismissive *yes, of course* or an honest *not at all*. He had the book on his lap, ready to start our reading, but he just stared at the floor. Or maybe at his own feet. I wanted to keep asking the right questions. He had always spoken with me honestly, but it was never quite so candid. He was talking to me like an adult, breaking all the rules I had come to understand about explaining death to children. He wasn't explaining death. He was explaining Charles Brozina, his father, and along the way, he was explaining James Brozina, my father, even more clearly.

"He worked hard every day of his life. Started working full-time when he was barely a teenager, after his father died."

I'd heard this before, but for the first time I actually tried to imagine my grandfather as a child, not much older than I was now, working to support a family. It made me exhausted just thinking about it. I felt even worse imagining his life without his father. What would have happened to my dad if Poppop had died while his children were still young? And how could my grandfather bond with his children after giving up his own childhood to work like an adult? Paying your son for a quick foot rub must have seemed silly, almost satirical, to a man who did manual labor for meager pay starting at age fourteen. But when I pictured his face, weathered and worn, it seemed happy. The skin seemed a bit gray and tough in my memory, but the mouth was set in a small smile. I had seen him alive just days ago, so I was sure this was right.

"He might have worked hard," I conceded, "but he died a happy man."

"Do you think so?"

When his voice came out, it sounded strangely like mine whenever I asked this question. Hopeful and looking for a reason to be optimistic, but in need of a little coaching. I wasn't quite sure how to play this role, since I was always on the other end of the conversation. But I tried to imagine what my father might say to himself. I kept my voice steady and confident.

"Yes, of course. He had four great children, who all have steady jobs and families now. He had grandchildren who loved him. He had Grammom"— here my father looked concerned, so I immediately smoothed over with— "who will miss him but had lots of great years with him. And he had a beautiful garden full of delicious foods, and a great pair of overalls, and a very memorable smell. He was a great man, and he lived a great life, and I think he died happy."

And then, to show I'd really been listening,

"Maybe we can look at some of those baseball cards you got with your foot rubbing nickels after Read Hot?"

The words reminded him we had a task at hand, and he pulled the bookmark out.

"You could write a person a pretty good eulogy, Lovie."

His voice and smile told me that he was feeling better, but I hoped his comment meant that he hadn't regretted being honest with me. Losing someone is sad. It was sad for both of us, even though he was an adult and my father. Had he told me this, I might not have believed him. But when he had spoken plainly and openly, I caught a glimpse of a rare, vulnerable side of my father that I would not truly see again for years. Maybe I was still too young to completely understand death, but I was old enough to realize that what had just happened was special, and that in my own way I had actually helped my father through the grieving process.

When he began reading, I snuggled even closer into his arm. I cried softly, my tears trickling down onto his shirt and his pillow, because I missed my grandfather. And I knew that was okay.

CHAPTER TEN

Day 829

It has long been an axiom of mine that the little things are infinitely the most important.

—Sir Arthur Conan Doyle, "A Case of Identity," *The Adventures of Sherlock Holmes*

The nurse knew my tricks. It wasn't that I didn't like school, or even that I particularly liked going home. There's nothing interesting on television between nine in the morning and two in the afternoon. But I liked going to the nurse, and I liked being sent home. It was a chance to practice my acting skills and maybe miss some multiplication drills at the same time. And the nurse was friendly, chatty, and warm. Even when she didn't send me home, she kept me in the office for a while. I think she enjoyed our visits almost as much as I did, and for the same reason: it was a break from the daily routine.

My teachers quickly caught on and started limiting my

nurse passes, but there were ways of getting around this. Substitute teachers, for example, were particularly sympathetic to a gravelly cough or clammy hands (I just so happened to have the latter naturally, and often used it to my advantage). The aides on the playground would send anyone in who asked, reasoning that you had to be feeling pretty lousy to willingly give up your kickball or dodgeball privileges. I hated, and will probably always hate, any of the games involving kicking, catching, or, in my case, hiding from bright red playground balls. I was bad at all of these "sports" and found them boring, but more importantly, I got hit pretty often. The aides didn't pick up on this, though. A quick point to my stomach, some light panting, and maybe a comment about how sad I'd be to miss my turn ("Oh man! I was really looking forward to kicking this dangerous-looking ball in the general direction of the opposing team!") and I'd be on my way back in the building, nurse's pass in hand.

I'd come in, and she'd smile and pull out a chair. Most of the time she would ask me what was wrong, but sometimes she'd try to guess from my facial expression or my posture.

"Sore throat, huh?" she'd say, reaching for a cough drop.

"Uh-huh," I'd whisper, quickly moving my hand from my stomach to my neck. "Really bad."

For the first ten minutes or so, I always had to go lie on the cot. There were three cots in the nurse's office, but I always chose the same one—my home away from home as my father might say—in the back left corner. It was in its own tiny, enclosed room, made of those shiny manila bricks popular in freshman dorms, hospitals, and other generally unhappy places. On the far end was a bathroom, which I avoided at all costs since some genuinely sick kid had almost certainly thrown up in there in the past few hours. The trick was to *act* queasy, not *get* queasy. After closing the bathroom door to avoid accidentally seeing a spot of half-digested chicken patty the janitors had forgotten to clean up, I climbed up on the cot and closed my eyes. It was impossible to sleep, partly because of the scratchy white paper rolled out over the cot and partly because of my age. At ten years old, I was still danger-ously close to the days of forced naps. My rebellious nature would barely let me take a long blink while the sun was out, let alone a voluntary snooze. But the point here wasn't sleep-ing, anyway—sometimes staying up was more convincing.

"Couldn't sleep a wink, huh?" the nurse would say, stand-ing over my cot twenty or so minutes after she sent me to lie down.

"Uh-uh," I'd say, shaking my head wearily.

"That throat of yours must be pretty bad, huh?"

"Uh-huh," I'd say, wincing as the words came out.

"Let's go call someone," she'd say, helping me to my feet.

"Oh no," I'd whisper hoarsely, "I was hoping to get back outside in time to kick the ball. I love kicking the ball, and having it thrown at me. But if you really think we should call home..."

Protesting, of course, always sealed the deal. I think because she believed that a woman's place was with her chil-dren, the nurse always called my mother first, even though she'd already moved out. I went to her apartment sometimes, but about halfway through the year, between her own illnesses and mine, my mother was usually out of sick days. The nurse's phone was always loud enough for me to hear the conversation on the other end of the line, and when I heard that tone in my mother's voice—regretful but sort of annoyed—I knew what was coming next.

"No problem at all," the nurse would say cheerfully. "I'll call her father then."

It wasn't that I didn't enjoy spending time with my father—of course I did, almost always. But once he'd gone to work, crisply dressed in a well-ironed dress shirt and pants and a colorful tie, he was a different man. At home he would indulgently tolerate my meaningless ramblings for hours at a time. We'd eat ice cream, and watch '50s horror movies, and, of course, read. But at work, only one of these mattered: reading was the focus of every moment, and anything else was a distraction.

My father spent thirty-eight years as an elementary school librarian, and I can say almost without bias that he was clearly the best around. His students loved him because he was good at what he did—from reading, to discipline, to creating a general mood of mutual respect, my father was an expert at getting children to love their time in the library. He was an absolute pleasure to watch almost any given day. On certain days, though, it bordered on cruel and unusual punishment.

On the rare occasion that my father was called to pick me up and actually agreed to come, I had to be genuinely sick—unlike the nurse, he automatically assumed I was faking unless there was a high fever involved. We'd make a quick stop at home to get my sleeping bag, pillow, and cough drops and then head straight back to his library. I tried to explain to him that when you are sick, really sick, the last place you want to be is in an elementary school surrounded by loud, potentially germy kids. In fact, that was precisely the environment I was trying to avoid by calling him to get me. But my father, who was born with only 25 percent of his hearing, could be particularly good at ignoring my protests when he wanted to. As long as I was physically able to walk up the stairs of his building, it was off to the library with me.

When we first arrived, it took him a few moments to notify the staff that he was back in the building and library classes could resume as usual. During this time I would spread out my sleeping bag behind his desk, a spot I thought hid me from view to some extent and led to less staring from his classes. You could still see me through the bottom of the desk, though, and I was perfectly clear from the side when you first entered the room. It really wasn't much of a hiding place. As soon as children came into the library, they immediately started asking who was behind the desk, wondering if I was in time-out or perhaps dead. My father ignored these questions completely, not wanting his students to be distracted any further, and whisked them to their seats.

Depending on what time of day I arrived, I would hear the same books anywhere from three to eight times. Each collection was a series of seven or so picture books, all classics in my father's eyes and almost all familiar to me from readings at home. He had the books completely memorized from hours of rehearsal, so he held the pictures facing the children the entire time. From cover to cover, he would recite, in a clear but theatrical voice, stories from the Berenstain Bears to folk-tales, and his favorites like the Clifford books or the Dumb Bunnies, never once stumbling or stopping, always keeping a set tempo and turning the pages at the appropriate moment.

Since I never came in during the first few weeks of the school year, I didn't know for sure if his students were, at one time, surprised by this technique. It certainly didn't surprise me—after seeing his rehearsals so many times, it took me years to convince myself that those who did not read to children this way weren't flat-out lazy. It seemed natural to know what was coming next, to turn the page with absolute certainty, to lift your eyebrows in surprise at an event you certainly knew was coming. As someone who was already writing and per-forming in plays with friends, this may have been where I first found my inspiration. My father claims that he could never enjoy acting, yet he did it every day for years, calmly chang-ing his voice to portray a small child like Dr. Seuss's Cindy Lou Who, or dramatically slamming the book shut at the end of a creepy tale like *The Monster and the Tailor*. It required skill, and lots of it.

But on those days, crouched behind the desk in my sleeping bag with a pounding headache or a churning stomach, I found his performances anything but impressive. With each gasp from the children at a surprising twist (which I couldn't even see, since the pictures were pointed at them and away from me) I groaned and covered my ears, retreating deeper into my sleeping bag, looking for somewhere, anywhere to hide from the noise and the lights. However bad I thought it was the first time, it got exponentially worse with the recitation of each book. Even worse was if the book rhymed, making it easy to memorize. In those instances, I'd find myself whispering along by the end of the day, unable to tune out my father's resounding voice, unable to sleep through the enthusiastic clapping that followed each and every book. During those moments, I would have given anything to be back on the cot in the nurse's office, in the dark brick room, perhaps actually napping for once.

During the car ride home, I'd make my case once again.

"The thing is I just feel worse when you take me to the library. It's loud and hot and there are people everywhere. It's not the kind of place you should take a sick child."

"For someone who is supposed to have a fever of 101, you're awfully clearheaded in making your arguments."

"Does that mean you actually understand what I'm trying to say?"

"Martha said, 'No discussion!'" he would repeat, reciting a classic (well, classic to us) line from the George and Martha picture book series by James Marshall. When Martha, or my father, said no discussion, it was final. I'd sulk all the way home, trying to pick the library floor dust out of my hair. Reading was his passion, so all-consuming that he could not be convinced to stop even to stay home with a sick child. He never took sick days himself, and he clearly could not see the point in sitting around on the couch doing nothing while I slept in my bed upstairs. If he was well enough to read, he would read, regardless of any distractions like my incessant cough from the back of the library.

This may be, in part, why The Streak worked. Nothing

stopped my father from doing what he had planned to do, especially when the thing he had planned to do was reading. Reading was sacred, traditional, perennial. I could hardly remember when the reading began (we'd read for years before officially starting The Streak) and I certainly couldn't imagine where it would end. Neither could he.

On those days when I curled up in my sleeping bag, counting the minutes and crawling deeper at the sound of any dangerous-sounding cough or sneeze from a fellow infection carrier, we still read. Of course we still read. Those five or more hours of nonstop, unavoidable reading in the library did not count. My father had not been reading directly *to* me, and it was in his eyes an unacceptable substitute. So after my bath, right before bed, I'd go get the Raggedy Ann doll he'd gotten me when I was four years old. She seemed big, almost as big as me, and she felt heavy when I was tired, but the bright red thread that outlined her smiling mouth made me feel better. I'd slip under the covers next to him, box of tissues in hand. I'd sneeze, and cough, and sometimes coil up tightly in an attempt to keep my dinner down, but we would read. We would read, just the two of us, like we always did.

CHAPTER ELEVEN

Day 873

To observe attentively is to remember distinctly.
—Edgar Allan Poe, "The Murders in the Rue Morgue"

It's got a great coat of paint, and it rides like a dream," my father began, trying to defend his purchase against the suspicious glance I shot him over my breakfast. This one did look like it was in great shape, but when my father brought home his sixth yard-sale bike of the summer, I knew we needed to talk.

"Listen," I began, "do you even know how to ride that thing?"

"Of course I know how to ride it," he said, wheeling it quickly past me and toward the basement door.

"And do you *plan* to ride it? Because if it's going to just sit in storage under the house like the others, you really should have saved your money."

He tilted his head to the side as if he couldn't quite hear me, mostly because he knew I was right. He was raised in poverty and generally took every purchase quite seriously. If there is one thing you can make my father feel guilty about, it's spending money.

"How much was it?"

"Twenty-five stinking bucks! A steal!"

"It's not a steal if you're never going to use it. Once you put it down there, is it coming back up? Will this 'steal' ever see the light of day again?"

"I was thinking maybe you could use it?" he suggested hopefully.

"You know that I have no idea how to ride a bike."

"We could try after you finish your slop."

There was his favorite word for food. I usually paid no notice to the term, but since the new frozen breakfast bowls we were trying weren't particularly appealing, I quickly lost my appetite.

"I'm done, but I'm not interested in learning. You're going to lose your patience, and I'm going to fall and crack my head open."

He stepped out on the porch for a moment, and then came back in carrying a bright pink helmet.

"I got this too," he admitted sheepishly.

I had absolutely no desire to ride a bike. I had gone twelve years without using one and I was doing just fine. My sister had learned to ride pretty well, but she still hadn't been allowed to leave the driveway. I'm not sure what my father was afraid would happen to her on our sleepy street, but all she was allowed to do was peddle to the mailbox, turn around, and peddle back. If he was outside, washing the car or pulling weeds, she was permitted to go the edge of the property next door and peddle back, as long as she didn't linger on the street. Needless to say, she lost her interest in riding at a young age, and I never quite developed mine. But I knew why this meant so much to my father, so I let him hold the back of my seat as I peddled in wobbly circles.

That didn't mean I couldn't bring it up, though.

"You know," I said, "no matter how many bikes you buy as an adult, they will still be your adult bikes. It's not like you can go back in time and give one to your ten-year-old self. And giving one to me doesn't count either, especially if I don't want it."

The comment seem to spur him on rather than deter him.

"Do you even know the story of my quest for a bike?"

"Well, kind of," I said, knitting my eyebrows as though I was in deep thought. Of course I remembered, but I liked hearing anything about my father's childhood.

As great as he was at reading, I thought he was even better at telling stories from his own life. But maybe I just cared about the main character in his a little more. We'd just started the Harry Potter series, which we looked into because it was the hottest thing on the market at the moment and kept reading it because I insisted. I completely understood why Harry wanted to know everything about his father and mother. I had an advantage over him, sure, because my parents were still alive and therefore not quite as mysterious. But it was still interesting to imagine what these big people were like as little people, whether they'd been horribly murdered by Voldemort or they were still alive and well, buying large quantities of used bicycles. And though my father was never a great wizard, his stories were just as interesting to me. Harry made me appreciate those stories even more, and I was in the mood for one.

"You had this bike that you were crazy about, that your parents got you when you were really little, right? A red one?"

I pretended to really believe this, although I had just thought it up on the spot. My father shook his head as though he felt sorry for me.

"Lovie," he said, "your memories are more cracked than mine are."

"I guess I don't remember," I said, knowing that he was falling for it.

He cleared his throat, pushed hard on my seat, and increased my speed a little.

"I wanted a bicycle," he began. "And I think your uncle Charles had one that Poppop found on the side of the road, but he got it because he was the oldest."

"Like primogeniture," I added, helpfully.

"Yes, because he was the oldest son. Did you learn that in Mr. C's class? It was like that but it was a bicycle and not land, and it had never belonged to my father. So actually it wasn't much like that, but that's still a good term to know."

My father, a history major because the library certification called for only one class when he was in college, was pleased.

"But Poppop didn't find two, you know, and there was no question of asking for one. Of course I wouldn't ask for one."

He pushed air out through his lips, probably wondering

if he needed to remind me why he couldn't have asked for one. But he had told me the stories of his family's extreme poverty—vegetable soup for dinner every single night, no hot water in the house, two stained shirts to last him the first year of high school—often enough to consider the point made. He didn't ask for anything because he wouldn't get it. He continued, "So whenever the neighborhood boys went somewhere, I would run alongside their bikes."

I wondered if he looked how he did just then, trotting beside me as I peddled too slowly to earn his full run, watching closely to see if I was leaning to one side.

"Everyone had a bike but me. Which I guess probably was good for my health, what with all the running. But it did make me stand out."

"Well, standing out isn't so bad," I reminded him, knowing that he prized individuality even more than I did.

"No, I stood out in a bad way. And I knew it. So when the Cub Scouts said they would have a citywide contest, and the top prize was a bicycle, you can imagine how excited I was. I was determined, absolutely determined, to sell the most chocolates. They were two for a penny, big chocolates with coconut cream filling, and whoever sold the most got the bike. I wanted that bike."

"Did you think you had a shot?"

"I *didn't* think. If I had a plan, it was just to work and work and work. I didn't give a second thought to what the other guys were doing, because my mind was made up to win the prize."

He leaned away from me for a moment, mistakenly thinking that I was balancing my own weight. I leaned toward him and he caught me and straightened me out without even needing to take a break from the story.

"It was late in the fall and it was nice and cold, and windy, every night after school. The kind of weather where your nose runs all the time, you know? Well mine would, in that cold. I wheedled Grammom to let me use Charles's bike, though generally I wasn't allowed to touch the thing, even if he wasn't using it, because it wasn't mine."

Here he looked longingly at the bike I was on, seeming to forget that it, like the five in the crawl space, was his.

"So I went every day after school, with those chocolates in the bicycle basket, riding to every house in a two-mile radius, hawking these lousy two-for-a-cent candies. Back then people were at home, because there wasn't anywhere to go. I would go out each and every night, trying to get rid of these god-awful chocolates—"

"Were they that bad?"

"No, actually they were tasty. I couldn't afford to eat my own product very much, but I remember that they tasted good, so I must have tried them at some point. The whole experience was unpleasant, though, so it makes the chocolates seem a lot worse."

"Did people buy any?"

"Not much, but I kept at it. Anyhow," he continued, "the time for the sale ran out and I went to the council meeting like I was meeting my destiny. There were boys there from all over the city, and the room was filled, and I mean *filled*, with Cub Scouts."

"How many?"

"At least a hundred."

I always made a point of asking this but the number never changed, so I knew he wasn't exaggerating.

"They quieted us all down and the scoutmaster said, 'How many of you have sold five dollars' worth?' There were quite a few. So he asked who had sold ten, and some hands went down. Which is understandable, because that was two thousand chocolates! Then he said fifteen dollars, and that was a major blow. But when he asked who had sold twenty or more, it came down to just me and one other kid."

I wanted to pull over for this part, since it was the climax and I was having enough trouble staying upright, but I didn't know how to brake and didn't want to interrupt him to ask.

"So the scoutmaster looked at me, and then the other kid, and he asked me first: how much had I sold? I told him the truth, and with pride—twenty-three dollars and sixteen cents. Then he turned to the other boy and asked how much he had sold, and the boy said twenty-five-something."

Usually at this point my father described how his heart sunk, watching the bike wheeled out and watching the other boy roll it away. But today he just looked at me, on the new bike. I hoped he wasn't picturing me as the boy taking the prize he had worked so hard to get.

"There was no second prize?"

"Not even a ruler. The other boy got the bike and I got nothing."

Here I had to confess my knowledge of the story.

"But he didn't really earn it, though, did he?"

"I can't say I know for sure. Years later, though, I found out that boy was the scoutmaster's son, *and* that he had a reputation as sort of a lazy bum. And then when you think about it, doesn't it seem a little convenient that the scoutmaster asked me how much I sold first? Don't you think his son was just going to say whatever was higher? At the time, I thought the guy had actually outworked me. But in hindsight, I think that's nearly impossible. Everyone would take his dad's word for it either way. I don't think that bike was ever really available as a prize. They always knew who would get it. I don't know, but that's just my gut feeling."

It would have been unlike my father, usually a bit cynical, to give someone who might have been corrupted the benefit of the doubt. But whenever I heard the story and pictured the boy and his scoutmaster father, I didn't trust them, either. I peddled faster, shaking them off.

"Then I started dreaming that I had a bike. I could see the bike clearly in my dreams. It was a sea-green color, with white sidewall tires, and a light on the front that you could switch on and off, and tassels at the ends of the handlebars. I would have these dreams quite often, every week and multiple times a week. In my dreams, I could see the bike, a Schwinn, out the window."

"And then what happened?" I asked, already smiling from ear to ear.

"And then that year for Christmas, my parents got me a bike! There it was on Christmas morning, right under the tree. It was exactly the way I had thought it would be in my dreams. Exactly."

My eyes watered every time.

"So you had described the dream to Grammom?"

"No! Not that I recall. Unless I was talking in my sleep."

"It was like a Christmas miracle."

He smiled and shrugged, and as he moved his arm I finally lost my balance and fell sideways onto the pavement.

"You clumsy she-ape!" he laughed, as he pulled me back up. My knees were already badly scratched, and the story was over.

"I still don't think I want to learn to ride," I confessed.

"That's okay, you'd probably break your neck anyway."

"But this is really a great set of wheels," I conceded. "And I don't think it was a waste of money."

After listening to his story again, I felt awful for scolding him earlier.

"Thank you for your permission to spend my money," he said, bowing low as though I were a queen.

"I think you should promise, though," I said, taking off my helmet, "that if I ever have a kid and he wants a bike, you have to give one of them to him. Your best one."

His eyes lit up.

"Oh, I'm sure that can be arranged."

"And maybe you should buy a few more, so he's got some selection."

"Yes, Lovie," he said, as we put the bike in storage next to its five brothers and sisters, "I think you're right again."

CHAPTER TWELVE

Day 1,074

Poetry needn't fix real life, Lou. It just need be. The fixing is up to us.

—David Baldacci, *Wish You Well*

I just don't understand what you're actually afraid of," my father said, as he looked in through my doorway for maybe the fifth time that night, "And I can't do anything for you if I don't understand."

I pointed at the bottom bunk without saying anything, tacitly insisting that he check it again.

"What am I looking for? What are you actually afraid will be there? His ghost? His spirit?"

"Don't make me say it," I whispered. "If I say it it's more likely to come true."

"Well, then it doesn't do a heck of a lot of good to call me in here. I don't know what I'm looking for. I'll tell you what's down here: a messy pile of blankets. Are you afraid of making your bed? Is that what this is all about? Because that's what I'd guess, judging by the state of things."

There are few things worse than being teased when you are scared, and there was only so much I could take. At twelve years old, this shouldn't have been a problem. But it was, and had been for long enough for him to know. Finally, I blurted out before he could make the situation any worse: *"I am afraid that JFK's dead body is on the bottom bunk! You know that! You check for it every night! Just tell me if it's there!"*

"Lovie," he said, "would I be talking to you so calmly if the body of an ex-president was lying on your bottom bunk? You don't think I'd be downstairs, calling the neighbors to come take a look?"

"No," I said, "you wouldn't, because it's unbelievable. That's what makes it so scary. You would be like the boy who cried wolf. No one would ever believe that his dead body was in our house."

"I think it would be an issue of national security if it was. We'd probably have to answer a lot of questions. And I get all mixed up when I have to answer questions, because my hearing's so bad. So for my sake, Lovie, do you think you could keep his body away for just a few more nights?"

"If I could keep him away, it wouldn't be for *your* sake," I whispered through the sheets.

It takes a certain type of child to develop a crippling, life-changing fear of the corpse of John F. Kennedy. I'm not sure what my parents did to raise that child, so I can't tell you how to duplicate the results. I do remember how it started, though, and it's not particularly terrifying.

I never had a bedtime ("If you wake up tomorrow and you're tired, you'll know you overdid it" was my father's motto), so it took me years to figure out the best sleep schedule for me. One particular night, maybe when I was around eight, I fell asleep quite early and had a nightmare. In the dream, I was on the playground at my elementary school, tossing a big red ball with my friends. Then my friends disappeared, and I started to walk back toward the school. I noticed that someone was following me and turned around to realize it was our former president John F. Kennedy. I told him not to follow me into the school because he was an adult, and also dead, and this was a school for children who were very much alive. But he still walked behind me, wordlessly, looking sad and sort of lonely. I felt bad that I couldn't let him in, and also scared that he wasn't listening to me. I don't like to be followed.

I awoke from the dream, which must have been short because everyone else in my house was still up and going about their business. I went downstairs to visit my dad and recount the dream, but he was distracted. He was working on some sort of paperwork and really needed to concentrate. To calm me down without occupying his time, he went to the shelf where we kept the videos and selected a documentary about JFK that made him seem like a sweet and caring man. He thought this would help me to understand that JFK wouldn't hurt me even if he could. He forgot, however, about the end of the film: a fifteen-minute montage all about

Kennedy's assassination and funeral. It was dark, and even creepier because the footage was in black-and-white. Death on such a national scale was a very big thing to such a small girl. I ran back upstairs and dove into my bed. Thus, a JFK-phobic was born.

To be completely fair, it was not the person himself whom I was afraid of, initially. I was afraid of his dead body, and I had somehow become convinced that it would appear one night on my bottom bunk, all laid out and ready for a funeral. I don't know where I got this idea, and I'm happy to report that today it makes me laugh. Then, though, it was a very grave and serious matter.

Every night, I would go through a huge ordeal to avoid the body. At first I tried going to bed while it was still light out, but because it was winter that only gave me an hour or so from the time I got home from school. And if I went to bed early, it meant waking up early, while it was still dark out. So the darkness was unavoidable. Instead, I tried turning on all the lights in my room and sleeping with them on. My parents didn't even yell at me, but finally the overhead light in my room burned out and I wasn't tall enough to replace it. My father was, but I think he made a conscientious decision not to do so. As I got older, contrary to my parents' expectations, the fear actually got stronger. By middle school, avoiding JFK's dead body, which was obviously lying in state on my bottom bunk, was the focus of my evening.

I brought one of my cats in and left him on the bottom bunk, not as a sacrifice but as a guard. The cats were very brave. Then I hopped up to the top bunk in one big step, putting my feet only on the middle rung of the ladder. Of course, if JFK's dead body was going to try to pull me down by my feet, he would have a prime opportunity while I was going up the ladder. I wanted him to know that I was on to his tricks. Once I reached the top bunk, I looked down every few minutes and called for backup (someone to make sure he wasn't tucked out of sight) every half hour until everyone but me fell asleep.

The fear soon shifted from JFK's dead body to JFK in general and included even photos of or quotes about him. So it was with great terror that I learned my father was planning a family trip for my sister and me shortly after my mother moved out, and one of the stops was the JFK Memorial Library. My father tried to convince me that I liked libraries more than I feared JFK. I had to point out to him that he did not know his own daughter, and that we'd visited before—it wasn't just a library.

No, it was worse: it was a museum *filled* with things Kennedy had used, or worn, or touched. There were things that belonged to Jackie Kennedy, too, my father reminded me, as he tried to pry my fingernails from the museum's gate. Fashionable, pretty things like outfits and hats. I had no interest in fashion. My interest was in self-preservation. I made it as far as a bust of Kennedy, shiny and golden to create a false sense of security, before retreating to the gift shop in tears. People stared. I wondered what they thought was going on. I found a bench in the book section and tried to steady my breathing.

After three tense hours, I finally heard my sister and father laughing about something as they approached. I curled up on the corner of my bench and hugged my knees to my chest, an act that I had always pictured made me look bigger, like a cat puffing out his tail and making his hair stand on end. Kath took it upon herself to mother me when no other females were around, and I could see as her eyes softened that we were going to have one of those moments. Feeling genuinely bad for me, she took a seat close behind me on the bench, patting my back and telling me it was okay. It was time to go anyway, she reminded me and the worst was over. I liked her technique. And because we are who we are, my father tried our usual fix: reading. He picked a book up off of a shelf near me. I had been eyeing the book curiously because it didn't seem to fit in with the others. There was no black-and-white portrait of the Kennedy family on the cover—instead, from the cover illustration, the book seemed to be about a goat.

"*Billy Whiskers,*" my father said, as he flipped open to a page at random, "They mentioned during the exhibit that this was JFK's favorite book as a child. Looks like it's not half bad, and it's on clearance. Should we get it and give it a try?"

I shook my head and looked away, but found myself looking back at the goat on the cover anyway. In such a fearsome environment, he didn't seem so bad. He had been my ally during my wait, the one thing in the store that, as far as I could tell before my father spoiled him, had nothing to do with John F. Kennedy. Now I felt bad for leaving him behind to fend for himself in this horror house of smiling photographs.

"Okay," I said, more to the book than to my father, "I guess we can give it a try. On vacation. But I know what you're doing, and it's probably not going to work."

What he was doing, specifically, was trying to use The Streak as a solution to a problem. It was something he did often, even if he wasn't doing it intentionally. There were just trends: after my mother moved out, we read stories about young girls without mothers. When there were bullies at school, we read about kids who outsmarted their nemeses rather than resorting to fistfights. And now, probably because there weren't any books about JFK-phobic middle schoolers, he was getting creative.

We took the book back to the hotel and moved Lois Lowry's *The Giver* into my father's suitcase. The story of a young boy being held responsible for the entire history of his people was intriguing, and the futuristic world they lived in was unbelievably believable. We were starting to see the flaws in the supposedly utopian world, and we'd left off on a cliff-hanger that made me beg my father to stay up just a little longer. That made it even harder to put the book down and pick up *Billy Whiskers*, so it's possible I went into the experience with more than a little bit of a bias. But we were spending only two nights away from home, and my father and I had agreed that if I liked the new book enough I would keep reading it on my own, and we'd go back to *The Giver* together as soon as we got back.

I don't remember much about *Billy Whiskers*. It must have been pretty decent because I did keep reading it once I got home. But the problem was that there was no safe place to enjoy it. My favorite spot to snuggle up with a book was in bed. I'd even set up a makeshift shelf that held a small lamp and a bookmark, so I could read until I got sleepy without having to jump down from the top bunk to turn off the lights. I couldn't bring *Billy Whiskers* up there, though. If JFK knew I was reading his favorite book, he'd want to come see for himself. If I left the book anywhere in my room, for that matter, he'd stop by to read it while I was asleep. Worse yet, he might stop by to read it while I was wide awake.

I tried keeping the book in the basement but decided that was a bad idea, too. That was just asking for it; it would be like keeping cheese on your doorstep and then wondering why so many mice were always coming to visit. Ultimately, I had no choice but to secretly put it in the lost-and-found box at school.

There are some things that reading, or The Streak, couldn't fix. *Billy Whiskers* was not, to my father's surprise, the answer to my fears. Even after I got rid of it, I thought JFK might be able to smell the ink on my hands. I washed myself in the bath that night with the zeal of Lady Macbeth herself. I ran into my room at full speed, trying my best to go straight past the bottom bunk without even looking at it, blurring my eyes to avoid even a peripheral glance. I hopped up and looked over, somewhat safe from my perch. Nothing. I read for an hour or two, forcing myself to get sleepy until my eyebrows felt like they were sliding down into my nose. Sometime after midnight, my father yelled for me to either turn off my light, which was shining directly into his room, or close my door. Of course, I couldn't close the door: that would mean getting out of bed. If I did, I'd have to start the routine all over again. So I peeked over the side of my bed one more time before switching off the little lamp, pulling the covers up over my head, and folding my feet under me so they wouldn't dangle over the sides.

I couldn't appreciate it then, but it takes creativity to lie shivering and shaking in your bed, wondering if your cats will know how to defend you, not against ghosts or the boogeyman, but against the immobile body of one of the most famous and beloved ex-presidents of the United States. Thanks to The Streak and my father, imagination was not something I lacked.

CHAPTER THIRTEEN

Day 1,206

Shutting my eyes tight, I try to erase that memory, but it plays over and over in my mind. And the strangest thing is I don't even remember what the argument was about.

—Kimberly Willis Holt,
When Zachary Beaver Came to Town

My dad is not an affectionate man. As a librarian, he told his students not to touch him, warning them that his skin was poisonous. Kindergarteners seemed to accept this as fact, but the older students often wondered why they couldn't just give their favorite teacher a hug. He does not like to be touched, and he does not want to touch other people. After school concerts or award ceremonies, I saw other parents hug and sometimes even kiss their children. My father considered it a bold and almost over-the-top display to stick one finger in my hair and scratch my scalp for a moment with his cracked fingernail, like he was helping me get an itch I just couldn't reach. If the event called for such a grand gesture, he would do it quickly and then back away several feet. This is not how I always remember him, though.

Before The Streak began and for the first few years, I had an assigned place for Read Hot: nestled in the crook of my father's arm, turned to the side so I couldn't see the pages (once I could read, it made him self-conscious to know that I was following along), trying my best to be a good listener. I was just inches from his ear, so any noise I made was easily detected. If the chapter was going particularly slowly or my mind was wandering, though, I was not the best audience. When I was younger and trying my hardest to be good in spite of distraction, I would chew my hair. It curled perfectly to fit inside my mouth, and the shampoo we used tasted like peaches. I would chomp and chomp, usually unnoticed by my father, but if I really started paying attention to the book and absentmindedly let the hair fall, it would get his attention.

"What is this wet thing on my arm?" he would ask, already annoyed at having to interrupt the reading.

"Hmm? I must have sneezed."

"Have you been licking your hair again? It already looks like a rat's nest—it doesn't need to look like you've been gnawing on it, too."

And then, because I didn't want him to think about the wet hair on his arm, I would have to stash it somewhere. Coincidentally, my mouth provided a great hiding place.

On other nights, though, I was not as quiet. When I was struggling with a song in choir, for example, I would find myself humming my part without even noticing it. Even worse, I was particularly sensitive to arguments with my sister and mother and would sometimes sob openly during the reading. He was never sure how to respond to this, especially since the problems that really got me going were never particularly important. I could handle even very adult situations with grace, but I hated fighting or being scolded, and I could sulk for hours after either.

"Are you crying, Lovie?" he might ask, looking very uncomfortable.

"Y-y-yessss."

He'd wince. Emotional displays were almost as difficult for him as affection.

"Would you like to tell me why?"

He never demanded an answer or pried. I could tell him, or not.

"M-M-M-Mom yelled at me. Sh-she says I can't b-b-b-bake at her apartment anymore because I make a m-m-mess."

"I'm sure you do. But you can bake here if you want."

"We don't have any pots and paaaans."

"Well, the heck with you."

This would make me cry even harder, even though he meant it as a joke.

"Is there something else you want to say?"

I was holding up the reading and not making much sense.

"N-n-n-n-no," I would whimper, curling into his arm and pulling my hair into my mouth.

When I cried during our reading, it was always because of an issue with someone else. I had trouble telling my father when he hurt my feelings. I felt silly and embarrassed, especially since he rarely came right out and apologized for whatever he'd said to upset me. So when his comments were really smarting, I would take a long bath and cry just a bit more softly than the sound of the running water, hiding until I could completely control my emotions. There was no point in crying during the reading if he was the cause for the tears. Then we would have to talk about it. It would be weird.

But one night, when I was twelve, we got in some kind of argument just before we went up to read. It bothers me now that I can't remember any of the fight, because it tells me how trivial it must have been. It was a spat at worst, but it was just before Read Hot and there wasn't time to take a bath, so I hadn't gotten the crying out of my system. When I headed up the stairs shortly after he did, my face was burning and my throat felt tiny. I had to gulp air to keep from getting dizzy, and my breaths were loud and painful sounding. I can't remember if I was angry or sad about the argument—probably both—but I knew that I was on the verge of tears, and I refused to let my father see how upset he had made me. I considered telling him that I had a nosebleed, or making any excuse not to come into his room, so that I could sob for a few exhausting moments and come back in, tired but capable of being in the same room with him. There wasn't time for that, though, because the reading was already close to his bedtime and trying to back it up might cause another fight. I came in, but I was not in the mood for the usual routine.

As I crossed the room, I grabbed a pillow from our pile of spare bedding. I climbed onto his bed and planted the pillow firmly on the farthest edge from him, where my mother used to lie when they were still living together. He did not seem to notice, so I made a point of dramatically pulling the covers around me and rolling on my side, so that my back was toward him. I heard his head move, and he must have looked at me then.

There was a long pause. I could feel his eyes on my back, and I waited for him to say something. Would he actually yell at me, command me to roll over and put my head on his arm? It wouldn't be like him, to demand affection or even acknowledge that it had become the norm. The silence, and his stare, made my ears hot. I bit down hard on my hair, knowing he couldn't see it. If I had been sad, I was angry now, and I was proving a point. He took a breath as if about to say something. I scrunched up my face as hard as I could, determined to defend my position no matter what he said. But then he closed his mouth. He took a deep breath, opened the book, and began reading.

I had not expected him to let it go without comment, though I suppose I should have. There was nothing for either of us to say, or nothing that either of us *would* say, so ignoring it wasn't even out of character. His reading seemed faster than usual, and I suspected that he was as upset as I was. We would never break The Streak intentionally—even my rebellious side didn't consider this an option—we just both wanted the reading to go as quickly as possible so that we could retreat to our own corners and feel our own feelings.

What seemed like a twenty-minute chapter took less than fifteen, but those fifteen minutes were some of the hardest of The Streak. From the moment I put the pillow down on the opposite side of the bed, I somehow knew that I was never coming back. I was already a preteen, and my friends seemed to think it was strange enough that my father still read to me every night. I had never told them that I usually listened curled up against him, resting on him and feeling the words vibrate through his chest. This would have seemed very strange, especially from a family that didn't even hug. Now that I was lying across from him, finally using up some of the space on the queen-size bed, it seemed logical. A twelve-year-old girl belonged here, on her own side of the bed with her own pillow. And besides, even if I wanted to go back to his arm tomorrow night, how could I? It would seem like an apology, or a truce, and I was not ready for either. The time would never be right to move back. I had a new reading spot.

But as I lay there considering this, and being sure to get all the peach flavoring out of my hair, I realized that this was much more sad than the fight itself. I was hurt, and I needed space. I could not just roll over, snuggle up to him, and pretend nothing had happened. But I was aware, painfully aware, of what I was giving up. We had no physical contact, almost without exception. Scrunching up between his elbow and his arm was the only closeness we had, but it was much closer than most fathers got with their almost-teenage daughters on a regular basis. Giving up my spot meant giving up the only opportunity my father had to be touched by another person. No one tried to hug him anymore, knowing he wouldn't allow it. Somehow, my spot had gone for years without mention. Pulling back drew sudden attention to it and made us both think, I assume, how strange it was that the tradition had even lasted that long. It was something neither of us had ever really considered, and now that we were thinking about it, it seemed awkward and forced, even though it never had been. It would be now.

I curled up into a tight ball, feeling angry and guilty at the same time. If he hadn't yelled at me I would be lying on his arm right now, and maybe neither of us would have realized how strange the tradition was until I was fifteen or sixteen. I could have had years left of smelling his soft cotton undershirts and staring at the hair on his arm, but I ruined it, or he ruined it, and now we couldn't go back. I dug my fingernails into my knees under the covers in an effort to stop the tears, but they came quickly and started spilling down my chin, onto the blankets. I tried not to make any noise, but I had to blink so quickly to get the tears out that my eyelids actually made a sound, a wet and sad sound that seemed much louder than my father's voice. And I knew that my breathing was becoming even more uneven. I hated, absolutely hated, to cry about anything to do with him in front of him, but if I couldn't help it, I could at least try to hide it. I coughed loudly, hoping he'd think my sniffling was just a cold.

When he finished reading, he put the book down beside the bed and just lay there quietly. I think he wanted me to say something, but instead I covered my face with my wet hair and bolted from the room. I meant to make an excuse about needing to use the bathroom but forgot as I rushed past him and out into the hall. I wanted to go to my room and crawl under the covers, but it was too close to his, so once again I made my way to the bathtub. The water pressure had been especially low, so the tub filled very slowly, which meant I would have plenty of time to get my feelings out. Even at this point, I could not clearly remember the fight. Mostly I remembered the quiet. He wanted to say something and he wanted me to say something, but since neither of us would say we were hurt, there was nothing for me to do but take a long, sad bath and feel horrible about what I'd done.

As I had imagined that night, I never did find my way back into his arm. I considered it the next night, but it seemed like too much of a gesture, and I was scared that he might want to talk about what had happened the night before. I felt more comfortable on my side of the bed, at least temporarily. Once a week or two had passed, he stopped expecting me to come over. He held his arms close to his sides. There didn't seem to be a place for me, and I felt too old to ask him to make one. So I stayed where I was, missing the closeness but still listening.

I listened, and he read, and somehow we made it work.

CHAPTER FOURTEEN

Day 1,384

So we grew together, like to a double cherry, seeming parted, but yet a union in partition; two lovely berries molded on one stem.

—William Shakespeare, *A Midsummer Night's Dream*

There's hardly anything memorable about the day my sister left for college. It feels like there should be something to it, since it was an important event, but there's no big story. There wasn't an emotional scene or a heart-to-heart pep talk the night before. We were already good at good-byes; this one didn't even stand out. Just one more, like the rest. It all started years before.

Kath wanted to leave before she'd even graduated from high school, and we couldn't stop her. Other than family, my sister honestly wouldn't miss much by being away from home. We were living in strained conditions. My father wanted to get us out of debt, support the family while saving up for college educations, and keep the house—a nearly impossible combination on a teacher's salary. We survived, but not comfortably. My back-to-school wardrobe one year consisted of one orange shirt, a size too big and oddly stained, that I found on clearance. We went for a few years without eating any meals out, and even the occasional treat of two items each from the McDonald's Dollar Menu was enough to make my sister and me stare at each other bug-eyed, wondering what had come over our father to prompt such frivolous spending. My father was not being cheap; he was doing what he thought would work. And all of this paired with our parents' separation left things almost as tight and strange at home as they were when we were all fighting under one roof. It wasn't as bad as some families had it. To me, it really wasn't bad at all. It wasn't a reason to leave.

That was not why my sister left. She wanted to see the world, and she was beautiful with languages. I thought she made them up out of her head, plucked them out of the sky and strung sounds together to make words that somehow others understood. One night, when I was very small, she sat on the bathroom counter while I was in the tub, teaching me phrases that she swore I could say to someone a million miles away and be completely understood. I laughed at all the strange noises.

So when she announced, when I was in middle school, that she wanted to be a foreign exchange student, my father and I weren't even surprised. We'd had an exchange student already, for two weeks, and we thought it was a good experience. We encouraged her to go. Until she showed us the brochure. It was a one-year program, with no visits from parents and no breaks to fly home, not even at Christmas.

"A year?!" I said, "What could you do in Germany for a whole year?"

"Isn't this going to be expensive?" my father said. "You know we have no money."

My sister explained that it was actually free to students who qualified, and I stated firmly that I did not want her to qualify. Her feelings were hurt, but I couldn't let her go. Between my grandparents dying, my mother moving out, and my sister leaving, I suddenly felt like I was losing everyone. Kath was a steady, calming presence, even when she carried me around by my hair and teased me in front of my friends. I crossed my fingers that her interview would go poorly.

Of course, the girl who would later go on to study at Yale and get a competitive government job using her language skills aced her interview and got the scholarship. She was headed to Germany for one year, all expenses paid aside from spending money. My father promised to give her what we had, which wasn't much. I felt like Tiny Tim, hobbling after her, trying to convince her that even with no money our life wasn't so bad, and that our family needed to stick together now more than ever. It had nothing to do with that, or us, but it felt like it did. I couldn't even begin to imagine life without her.

We drove her to her orientation in Washington, D.C., knowing full well that we would be coming back without her. We played her favorite CDs in the car, and I put my head on her shoulder. I wished for us to get in an accident—nothing big, just enough to slow us down and make her late, so the director of the program would get mad at her and tell her to stay home. We were actually several hours early. My father is always early for everything, especially when making a first impression. We stopped at our hotel so that my father and I could check in and drop off our bags, but my sister kept hers in the car to take with her. It was going by too fast. Things got blurry and loud.

The convention center where my sister met her orientation group was actually quite lovely. It had dramatic, floor-to-ceiling windows and velvet carpets. The floors were a highly polished marble that clicked appreciatively whenever it was greeted by the professional grace of high heels. I begrudgingly admitted that the program had gotten something right. But the beautiful setting did not distract me from the fact that they were taking my sister away from me for an entire year. What did they need with Kath? She was an excellent student and a great representative of our country—all right, yes, but so were lots of other people. I needed her more. I did not let the lobby impress me.

Some meet-and-greet activities were scheduled to acquaint the students with each other and their families. They encouraged us all to laugh and smile and make silly jokes, which seemed absolutely unfair. No one was in the mood for it— the students were too nervous and the parents were too sad. Actually, everybody was sad. They tried to pretend we were excited. I don't think a single person was. The students probably got excited some time after we left. The families never did. The activities were supposed to last longer than they did, but they slowed to a crawl and then stopped altogether. Everyone was wondering what would come next. When someone stepped before us to speak, I could see the strain in my father's face. We held our breath and wondered if this was it.

"All right, everyone, it's time to say your see-you-laters," the woman running the program said with a great big smile, as though she were telling us it was time for pie and ice cream.

"See-you-laters?" a parent near us asked. "What does that mean? See you later tonight? After dinner? What?"

The woman shook her head and scratched the back of her ear, trying to avoid eye contact. She'd done this many times, it was clear, but she had never quite figured out what to say at this point.

"You mean see-you-in-a-year. You mean that we should say good-bye," I said quietly.

The woman smiled that big smile again and nodded much too enthusiastically for the occasion. The crowd surged forward toward their children, sisters, boyfriends, and girlfriends in one motion, clumping together into a tight huddle. Kath was saying something, but we could barely hear her over all the crying and quick, fervent, insistent conversation around us. Boyfriends and girlfriends begging for faithfulness. Parents begging for levelheadedness, sobriety, and caution. Everyone begging, "Please don't leave me," even if they were saying other things and trying to look happy. To my surprise, my sister and father had a long embrace. Tears were streaming down her face. Then he started, and I couldn't help myself. I hugged Kath and smelled her hair. I kissed the light layer of foundation on her cheek, which I knew came out of a small green compact with a Nickelodeon sticker on it. She'd been mad at me when I put the sticker on, but she'd never bothered to take it off. I put her hand in mine, and she squeezed it and let go. She waved and walked around the corner. I stayed where I was.

For ten minutes, my father and I couldn't bear to leave the spot where we were standing. We didn't talk—we had enough work just mopping our faces dry only to find that they were immediately saturated before we'd even finished. I looked at him and wanted him to say something meaningful.

"At least we're still on the same floor as her" was all he said, his voice breaking.

We got into the elevator, and as the doors closed we cried harder, grateful for the privacy.

"At least we're still in the same building as her," I said.

The slow walk to the car and exit from the parking lot prompted my father to say, "At least we're still on the same street as her."

With each added distance, we had more and more trouble keeping ourselves together.

We got back to the hotel and sat on our beds for a while, looking at the walls and biting our lips.

"Let's go to the pool," my father said finally, searching his suitcase for swim trunks.

"Now? In our condition? I think we'll get some funny looks. I'm not sure I'm up for it."

"It's a big hole filled with water. No one will even see our tears. We'll blend right in."

"Or we'll raise the water level and flood the pool."

We went and floated on our backs, not talking or even moving. A year without Kath.

When we did our reading that night, it almost didn't seem right. Kath was leaving and we were just sitting in a hotel bed, reading *The Secret Garden* like it was any other night, like we were back at home and things were as normal as could be. The moment we'd both been waiting for since we began the book, the moment when Mary finally found the entrance and saw the garden for the first time, finally came. We turned the page and there it was, suddenly, in all its green and overgrown glory. But it was lost on us. It went by without a comment or even a gasp. The world of our books, which had always seemed very real and very close, seemed so tiny and distant. I felt a million miles away from Mary. Nothing she did really mattered. She could discover a garden or stay in her room and play checkers, for all I cared. The fact that she was also coping with loss—a different sort of loss, of course—didn't occur to me. Even if it had, it wouldn't have moved me. She was not real, and reality was weighing heavily on my chest, keeping my attention away from the garden where things had the potential to grow and get better.

"At least we're still in the same state as her," my father said, as we handed in our hotel key and headed for the parking lot the next morning.

And later, when we reached home, "At least we're still in the same country."

Two days later, her plane left for Germany. I wasn't even sure if we were under the same sky.

My father and I learned to live as just the two of us—an act we would later perfect. There were fewer expenses when it was just two people, anyway. As it turned out, my sister got a poor match for a host family and, after a series of strange incidents, including being asked to eat uncooked roadkill for dinner, she took an emergency flight home just in time for Christmas. But she never really came back. She stayed for a month and left again to join a new host family in Germany. Later she lived in Russia. Now she lives in Serbia.

So on her first day of college, a day when I was thirteen that I've been trying to recall, there's nothing much to remember. There weren't any tears. It was a huge day for the students and families around us, but we felt disconnected from them. They hadn't had the practice we'd had. They cried and we shrugged. Now she was only a car ride away. We could see her on weekends and holidays. College, it seemed to me, was a vast improvement. We carried the final boxes to her room with smiles on our faces, waved good-bye knowing it was really see-you-later, and saw her again in a week. My father did her laundry when she came home, and her clothes smelled like mine. Nothing was wrong with it. Then she left again for a semester abroad. She was always leaving, and I can't say I blame her. She had wonderful opportunities. She was never just running. I remember her leaving for lots of places, but not college.

Later, during our worst financial straits and while Kath was in Russia, my father kept the house at fifty-two degrees and went to bed wearing two wool hats and a pair of gloves. I also had a pair of gloves, called my typing gloves, with the fingers cut out to allow easier work on school projects. A friend left my sleepover because she was too cold. It wasn't pretty. I wondered what my sister was doing every day, and if it was warm where she was. We talked on the phone and she said no, it was even colder there, she missed us more than words could explain, and she would keep calling regularly. She did. Still, the days got shorter and something was missing. Whenever I heard my father putting toast in I fumbled out of bed as fast as I could, only to remember when I got to the bottom of the stairs that no one was chasing me to claim the coveted spot warming our hands over the toaster.

Sometimes I lay in her bed at night and counted the stars. Not the ones out the window, but the little glow-in-the dark ones all over her ceiling. We'd split a pack of them years ago, and most of mine had already fallen off, landing every now and then with a little plastic sound as they hit my floor or dresser. But Kath had used more tack than I had, and hers were still up, even after the cold winters and hot summers our house had come to expect. I wanted to peel some off and mail them to her, so we could look at them together every night, but they had lasted this long, so I let them stay. The real things, the burning balls of gas in the night sky, weren't enough. Everybody had those; these plastic stars understood and remembered. They'd seen it all. They were still here.

CHAPTER FIFTEEN

Day 1,513

For they said, it was a shame to quarrel upon Christmas Day. And so it was! God love it, so it was!
—Charles Dickens, *A Christmas Carol*

I am not putting that thing on my Christmas tree."

"*Your* Christmas tree? How do you figure that?"

"I paid for it with all the money in my sock drawer and I spent two hours putting it up. I would say that makes it my Christmas tree as much as it possibly can be."

My dad was circling the tree, looking for a place to hang his favorite ornament: a big gold box, taller than my hand and wider than most novels, with a holographic photo of Elvis Presley on it. There were tiny, painted buttons on the ornament, but it looked more like a radio that mysteriously had a screen than a television. When you tilted it, it revealed either a photo of an incredibly sweaty, chubby Elvis or a screaming-into-the-microphone, tired-looking Elvis. It could not have been more hideous, and I was fairly certain it was originally marketed as a gag gift.

"Look, it plays music!" my father said, pressing a button on the back of the ornament to produce a tinny, whining sound that was supposedly the song "Hound Dog" but sounded more like the animal itself howling and walking across a pile of bicycle horns.

"It is lovely, yes, no one can deny that. I am not denying that at all. But is there room for it?"

The answer was no—I had filled up every inch of the tree with ornaments. Some were homemade, some were family heirlooms, and absolutely none depicted fat, sweaty men. I planned for things to stay that way.

There was a knock at the door.

"My hands are full!" I yelled, organizing our presents so that the ones my father had wrapped in tinfoil weren't immediately apparent.

"I just got out of the shower!" my sister called from upstairs.

My father didn't notice the knock or chose to ignore it as he knelt down and tried to ascertain how far an ornament had to be from the ground to keep the cats from batting at it.

"Um, I guess I'll get it then," my sister's boyfriend, Nathan, said cautiously.

He and Kath were splitting up the college break between New Jersey and his home state, Texas. He had stayed with us few times before, including a couple of Christmases, but he was clearly uncomfortable answering the door in someone else's house.

"*Merry Christmas, everyone!*" my mother shouted before she was even inside. Her arms were overflowing with blankets and pillows, which she deposited on the couch before announcing that she had to go get her sheets and a few more pillows.

"Are you planning to sleep on a pile of jagged rocks?" my father called, as she headed back out to her van. "Because if you're not taking the couch, I'm going to use it to keep my presents comfortable."

Although my mother had stayed at her apartment during her first Christmas away, it didn't feel right to me. There was no reason for her to sleep alone, or wake up alone, on such a big day. So I suggested that she sleep at the house, just this one night out of the year, and the tradition continues to this day. My mother never complained about crashing on her ex-husband's couch, and my father never really questioned the idea of having his ex-wife stay in his living room. Although they can fight as bitterly as anyone at times, my parents have always maintained a friendship that goes beyond putting on a good face for our sake. My mother stayed over because she knew it was important to me, even though I was now thirteen years old, and my father let her because he didn't think she should be alone for the holidays. It wasn't until I was about to graduate from high school and my dad's then-girlfriend refused to accept the arrangement that any of us even thought of it as out of the ordinary. To our surprise, he defended the tradition even then.

"Nathan, before you go upstairs," I said, grabbing him by the sweater, "tell me this: how do you think baby Jesus would feel if he knew there was a hip-shaking, rock-and-roll singing man at the top of our tree?"

I pointed at the ornament in question, which was now hanging where the star had been just a moment ago.

"I can't imagine what he'd say," Nathan said, trying to avoid conflict, "since I have never personally met him, that I know of, and also since I am Jewish."

"But if you had to guess," I pressed.

"Well, didn't Elvis sing a lot of gospel music? I think baby Jesus would like that."

My father broke into "How Great Thou Art" and moved holographic Elvis back and forth for dramatic effect. Sweaty, chubby. Tired, screaming. Out of the thousands taken during the man's career, you'd think they could have found two slightly more flattering photos.

"What are we singing about?" my mother asked with a huge grin, as she finished piling blankets in a stack that could have put the Princess and the Pea to shame.

"Are we singing about how this butter has been expired for six years?" Kath said, waving the box in my father's face. "Or is that not important to anyone but me?"

"That has been in the freezer since the week I bought it. It is perfectly good."

"This is why we never have company over. Dad, I have told you many, many times that the freezer does not stop the hands of time."

My father got serious.

"What is this, Christmas Eve or Complain About Dad Day? If you don't like the butter, don't eat it! What do I care? Was I begging you to eat it? Do you think I was crossing my fingers, just hoping that you would come down and eat some toast and tell me what I am doing wrong with my life?"

"She would have started with your taste in ornaments," I interjected.

"James, I'm sorry, but is this present for me?" my mother called over all of us, waving a tinfoil-enrobed box above her head. "Because if it's the slippers I asked you for, I'd like to open them now."

"It is not for you! Can't you read tags?"

He took the present and moved it to the back of the pile, apparently annoyed that she'd revealed its shape and texture in front of the true recipient, whoever that was.

"I'm so sorry, Jamie! I really am! I thought I was 'To Whom It May Concern,' honestly, I did!"

From where I was standing, helping my sister check the expiration dates on everything else in the refrigerator, I could just barely make out the tag, which read, *To: Whom It May Concern. From: None Of My Business.*

It was a typical James Brozina tag, but even I didn't know what it meant. I had a feeling that it was for Nathan, though, because my father had drawn a dancing man on the tinfoil in Sharpie. Actually, that didn't narrow it down at all.

My mother turned on some Christmas music, and everyone but my father sat around the tree to talk and admire our decorations. My dad headed to the dining room, turned on the television, and watched the news while eating a peanut butter sandwich. He wasn't being antisocial—he enjoyed watching the news and eating peanut butter sandwiches, and he liked it just as much on Christmas Eve as he did during the rest of the year. And since Christmas cheer meant letting everybody appreciate the holiday in his or her own way, we let him enjoy himself uninterrupted.

My father had read to me earlier in the day so that I could better enjoy the Christmas Eve festivities. We were working on Gary Paulsen's *Hatchet*, but we'd put it down for the night. The tale of a young boy surviving on his own in the wilderness was an exciting read, and it had become even more exciting when I realized my lab partner just so happened to be reading it, too. Zack and I would go back and forth, imagining what we would have done in each situation and arguing the plausibility of each other's schemes. I enjoyed the book very much, but on Christmas Eve it didn't quite seem festive enough, so we'd traded it out to read a collection of out-of-order paragraphs from *A Christmas Carol*. I liked to read the passages about Scrooge's sister Fanny, even though they were sad, because she sounded like such a nice person. And then to cheer us up we read about the party at the Fezziwigs', a name that instantly makes me smile just from the sound of it.

Because our reading was done, my dad went to bed first. The rest of us stayed to shake our presents and drink more hot cocoa, which I happily gulped even though I hate hot drinks. Christmas can change your opinion on most anything. When we got up to go to bed an hour or two later, I instinctively reached to remove the Elvis ornament and replace it with the star we always used.

"For what it's worth," Nathan said, standing behind me, "I would leave it, if I were you."

"Are you looking at the same holographic gold box that I am?" I asked in astonishment.

"Yes."

"And you think it is attractive?"

"No, not exactly."

"Well, what?"

"It's a silly ornament. It's even sillier at the top of the tree, where a star or an angel might be, if this were some other family. But one thing I've always liked about this family is that it is always fine to be silly. It's none of my business, but I don't think this tree stands out in a bad way. It's just right for the Brozinas, when you think about it."

"You're making me feel like Charlie Brown," I said, "with my pathetic but appropriate Christmas tree."

"What's wrong with Charlie Brown?"

"What's wrong with our Christmas star? The one we've used for years."

"Nothing," Nathan said. "Nothing at all. Both are nice. The tree will look great either way."

He wished me a Merry Christmas and went to bed.

Alone in the living room, I stared at the great big tree.

I pulled up a chair to stand on and tried the star on for size. It looked good. I tried the Elvis ornament on. It looked silly. But when I put the star on and hung the Elvis ornament over it, it somehow looked just right. So that was how I left it.

In my bed that night, I listened to all the sounds of the house. There was my father's quiet snore, rhythmic and peaceful. There was my mother's open-mouthed breathing, like she was puffing on a car window to fog it up before writing her initials with her finger. I could hear my sister and Nathan giggling, sounding sleepy but happy. From my feet, I could hear one of the cats purring.

Over the years, I had gotten used to living with just one other person. The house had stopped feeling empty, and I no longer minded the quiet. There is nothing wrong with being a family of two. But tonight, as our sounds blended together into a hushed Christmas carol, I savored the song, for once full and rich. We were singing something, and it was not "Silent Night." Maybe it was "Hound Dog." But I think it was an original.

CHAPTER SIXTEEN

Day 1,528

She tried to think of every pleasant and beautiful and wonder-ful thing she knew. She made a list of all the miracles in her mind. She recited poems to herself and sang softly all the songs she'd learned at school and all the songs Daddy sang. But it wasn't any good.

—Virginia Sorenson, *Miracles on Maple Hill*

A C is absolutely, positively, the worst grade you can give a person. It's worse than a D or even an F, because it means that you are, totally and completely, average. And you're not even average in the real-world sense, because most students either do well or do poorly. You either identify yourself as someone who gets good grades or someone who doesn't. If you get a C, that identity gets a little blurry—are you an underachieving smart kid, or an overachieving dumb kid? Also, if you're used to getting mostly As, a C is basically an F that took more work. Among the words that start with *c*: *crusty, canker sore, cannibal*, and *congeal*. I rest my case.

So it was no small blow when, after seven years of mostly

As (with scattered Bs in math and science), I received my first C. Worst of all, it was in my best subject.

Report cards were given out *in* homeroom, but not *during* homeroom: the last class of the day was cut short so students could make their way back to their first class. In high school, they gave them out during first period, but middle school students (including myself, as I would soon find out) were still prone to big, emotional scenes, and starting the day off with one could be disastrous. Just a few minutes before the final bell, I pushed my way through the crowds from my Spanish class to my geography class and took a seat near the front in hopes of getting out sooner.

I had places to be. I was in the school play and had plans to meet some friends first thing after school to run lines before rehearsal. There was no sense of anticipation, because my report cards were never a surprise: As in the subjects I liked, Bs in the ones I didn't. Sometimes I managed to pull out an A in math or science, but this hadn't been my year so far, and I wasn't expecting that. In fact, I didn't even look at the report card when my teacher handed it to me. I folded it over a few times so that it would fit neatly in my Trapper Keeper, threw everything into my backpack, and headed to meet my friends.

No one else had made it out as quickly as I had, so I had to wait around for a bit. I slouched against some lockers and had started looking through my bag for some candy when I remembered the paper in my binder. I fished it out, flattened the creases, and placed it on my lap. I enjoyed reading the teacher comments. But something else caught my eye first. I saw the curve, like a snake uncoiling and preparing to attack. A small, black, spiteful C. In English.

In English! I had to look again to believe it. My grades certainly could have slipped in biology, or pre-algebra. I was probably scraping the bottom of the B barrel in the latter anyway. But English was, and always had been, my best subject. I loved it. English was just stories—you wrote stories, or you read stories, or discussed stories. Essentially, I got a C in story time.

I stood up quickly, thinking it must be an error and planning to see the teacher before she left the school. Then I pictured the teacher, this one particular woman, and I knew it was no mistake

She wasn't exactly mean. Best described, she was cool. She never seemed particularly happy to be with her students or in her classroom. She had eyes that I always remember as being gray, but not the gray-blue of my eyes. They were silver, and cutting in their disinterest. She made sarcastic comments while she graded papers at her desk. She only smiled when she was making fun of something, and I don't think she actually liked books. I didn't like her, and she didn't like me.

This teacher and I had butted heads on numerous occasions that semester, mostly revisiting the same debate: did my creative interpretation of the assignment mean that I had not successfully completed it? She'd hand me a low grade because of something she thought I did wrong, like writing a poem as a reading response. I'd give reasons why I thought my work was acceptable, pointing out that I had met the required word length and reflected on the assigned reading. I'd talk, and she'd turn and walk away, and I usually assumed that I'd won the argument and she was going to change the grade in her book.

I guess that assumption was my big mistake. Those conversations hadn't changed anything, and now I had a C, my first-ever C, in my very best subject. I, the daughter of The Streak, had a C in English. Worst of all, one of the papers she'd given me a low mark on was on *The Giver*—a book I was reading for the second time in her class because my father and I had already devoured it at home and had lengthy discussions about it. I could practically recite passages from it, and I could make comparisons to other books we'd read together, and often did. I wasn't showing off—I was so excited about everything we'd read at home together, I couldn't wait to get my classmates hooked on the books I loved. If nothing else, I think that enthusiasm would have amused most teachers. But not this one. My background, and my passion, were meaningless. My father read to me every night, and I got a C in English. In *English*.

Right in the middle of the busy hallway, I felt my jaw begin to slack, which meant one of two things: I was either going to cry or throw up. Luckily, I suppose, it was the former. I stuck my head into my bag to make it look like I was searching for something and keep my face hidden, but my breathing was loud and heavy. Finally a security guard, who also happened to be my friend's mother, stopped to ask what was wrong. I showed her my report card. She handed it back.

"It's not quite as pretty with that one guy on there, but it's still a beautiful report card. Don't worry about what your dad will say. I'm sure he'll understand."

It wasn't that. Of course he would. I cried all the way through rehearsal, and when my father came to pick me up, I didn't try to hide it.

"*Look!*" I sobbed, as I flopped into the backseat. I thrust the paper forward and leaned my head against the back of the passenger seat. He read for a few seconds, and then let out a little gasp.

"What the heck?" he said.

"*I knoooooow!*" I wailed.

"How did this happen?"

"*She haaaates me!*"

We had discussed this woman many times before.

"Well, I doubt she's your biggest fan. I'm guessing you challenge her. But challenge can be a good thing, and any teacher worth her paycheck should know that."

I shook my head, pulled at my hair.

"You don't think I'm angry or anything, do you?" he said, before starting the car.

"Of course not. I'm just upset because it's upsetting!"

"All right. Because if you want, I can show you my report cards. They're in a box at home, and not a one of them is anywhere near this good."

"I know, I know, I know you're not mad. That's not why I'm crying. *I got a C in ENGLISH!*"

My voice broke as I gave way to sobs once more, and I wrapped my arms around my face as we left the parking lot in case anyone happened to be looking in the windows.

"Well," he said, "what can we do?"

"I don't know, nothing. Nothing in the world will help. Not one thing."

"What about Custard Corral?"

"That actually might be the one thing."

Despite the use of not one but two *c*'s in its name, Custard Corral was the solution to many problems. An ice cream stand a mile or two from my house, it specializes in both custard and goats. The goats are kept in a pen near the stand, and sticky-faced children often push half-eaten ice cream cones through the slots in the fence. Because of this, the goats are very friendly and also very chubby. Custard Corral is one of my favorite places on Planet Earth.

We got my usual—a strawberry shortcake sundae made with warm biscuits—and sat on a bench facing the goats. It made me feel a little better, but I felt silly admitting that ice cream could essentially fix even my biggest problems, so I didn't say anything.

"So do you want to tell me anything about the class?" my father asked.

"No," I said.

But I had been waiting all day to tell someone who would really understand.

"Well, it's just that her grading is so unfair. I always think I am doing extra work but she grades it like I am doing way less than everyone else. If it's a yes-or-no question, the grades are fair. But if it's a creative assignment or an essay, she can grade based on how much she likes you, and she doesn't like me very much."

"Yes," my father said, as he took a big spoonful out of my sundae, "there are plenty of teachers who do that. I see it happen all the time at work. It's a crying shame, but everybody plays favorites. Even the best of them—it almost can't be helped. Sometimes I do it without even realizing it."

I appreciated his honesty. I've never understood why parents try to convince their children that they've imagined a problem without even listening to the situation. Sometimes children feel ganged up on for no reason, but from my experience it's almost just as likely that the teacher is simply human and capable of making major mistakes. Kids can be quite perceptive.

"You're just used to being one of the favorites in English," he added.

"I think that is fair! If anyone is going to be the favorite, I mean. I work hard and I try new things and I think I ask good questions. I love reading and writing. What more do you want in a favorite?"

I stopped to take a big, comforting spoonful of strawberry goop and swirl around on my tongue before continuing with added gusto.

"And the stuff we read in class is way easier than the stuff we read at home. I try to talk to her sometimes after class about the books I'm reading with you. Like when we read *Island of the Blue Dolphins*, I suggested that she use it as assigned reading next year, because we'd liked it so much."

It was neither a "girl book" nor a "boy book"—Karana,

stranded on an island by herself for years on end, did things that would scare the manliest man. I offered to bring in our copy and read her some of it, and she didn't even pretend to be interested.

"I think she thinks I'm weird. If I were a teacher and I had a student like me, I would be happy. At least I think I would. Even if the girl was a little weird, it would still be nice. And I'm no good at math or science, no good at all. So when I'm doing the one thing I'm good at, I want someone to notice."

I realized that I'd risen up out of my seat as I'd explained, and I settled back down sulkily.

"*I* notice. You don't have to defend yourself to me, Lovie."

I had been done crying for almost half an hour, but when he said this, I started afresh. I had known he would believe me, but it was nice to know he believed in me. He couldn't figure out why I'd started again, so he just gave me a quick pat on the back and said, "If you don't gobble down that sundae in the next thirty seconds I'm going to eat the rest of it."

I handed it to him, and he poured it into his mouth like water.

I can't remember what we read that night, because I was still too upset to really concentrate on it. But I remember how comforting it was to lie there and let his words surround me, wrapping me up like a blanket and keeping out the cold. He believed me. He believed *in* me.

When I got to school the next day, my eyes still looked a little tired from crying. I took a seat next to my friend in homeroom and handed her the shameful document without even looking at it.

"Wow, a C, huh? What'd your dad do?"

"We went for ice cream. That's not the point; it's not about what he did."

"What are you talking about? Girl, if this were mine, my dad would have let me have it."

"Have what?"

"It's a saying. I would have been grounded. Man, he'd have been furious. You went for *ice cream*?"

"Yeah, I was upset so we went for ice cream and talked."

"I wish I had your dad."

"You aren't paying attention to the C, Shanelle. The C."

"No, I'm paying attention, all right. I'm paying attention to the fact that your dad actually cares that you are upset about a bad grade. He's upset that you're upset. Shoot, want to trade families for a bit? My mom makes really good deviled eggs."

She laughed, slapped me on the back, and handed me the report card.

"Count your blessings, girlfriend."

I counted: A friend like Shanelle. Ice cream. The Streak. And Dad.

I looked down at the C. It got a little smaller.

CHAPTER SEVENTEEN

Day 1,724

For animals and birds are like people, too, though they do not talk the same or do the same things. Without them the earth would be an unhappy place.
                    —Scott O'Dell, *Island of the Blue Dolphins*

You can pet him, the way a normal human might," I said, pushing Rabbi closer to my father.

"I am not touching that filthy creature with my hands."

My father's method of petting the cat *did* involve his hands, actually. But it was a sort of rough pinch—he grabbed a lump of the cat's fur, shook it, then grabbed another lump. Sometimes he would give Rabbi a light push onto his belly, to get him to stay in one place while my father showed his strange brand of affection.

"Why don't you try rubbing him, like this?"

I ran my hand over Rabb's back, gliding it softly across his fur until I got to his tail and then starting over again. We'd had the cats since around the time The Streak began, and by the age of fourteen I had practically earned a pet-petting merit badge. I had technique. I let my father try again, but he resorted to *his* old technique. I shook my head in frustration.

"Lovie, if he didn't like what I was doing, would he be purring as loudly as he is?"

I couldn't deny the sound, a loud humming that made Rabbi sound more like a motorized machine than an overweight, cross-eyed, half-Siamese cat.

"*And*," he added, "Would he come up every night if he wasn't getting something out of the bargain?"

Once again, he had a point. If you didn't count the Raggedy Ann doll my father had gotten me (despite my age she was still always in attendance, but she had no choice in the matter), Rabbi was the unofficial third participant in our reading streak. We usually read around the same time every night—between 9:00 and 9:30—so the pattern was predictable enough, even for a creature who didn't understand clocks. Rabbi had adjusted his sleep schedule accordingly; between eating and The Streak, he managed to stay awake for an impressive forty-five minutes a day.

As dedicated as he was however, he wasn't particularly interested in the reading itself. From Dickens to Shakespeare, we tried our best to come up with stimulating, appropriately challenging material, but Rabb still had trouble paying attention. Even when we read books involving cats, he simply could not make any personal connections with the text. He joined us, not out of a thirst for great literature, but because he needed his fix—what my father called his rubdown.

"You are miserable, Rabbi," he said to him almost every night after we finished reading, "You are a miserable, free-loading leech!"

I always thought this assessment was unfair. Yes, Rabb expected to be rubbed from the moment we started reading until my father turned out his light for the evening, and he didn't give anything in return. But as I pointed out to my father on many occasions, what *could* he have possibly done to show his gratitude? It was as though my father expected him to leap up after we'd finished petting him and go change his own litter before heading downstairs to organize the silver-ware and fix the leaky faucet.

The strangest thing about my father's insults, though, was that he always said them in a soft, loving tone. "You are a self-ish bum," was said in the same way a normal person might say, "I'm so glad to see you, please join us!" Of course, we all assumed this was what he actually meant, even though he argued otherwise.

"I never wanted these cats," he said, as he grabbed Rabbi's fur and shook it, making the whole bed vibrate with Rabbi's purring, "And now I have to pet them every night."

Actually, since our other cat, Brian, rarely came in for our reading, Rabbi was getting most of the affection.

"First of all, what you are doing is not petting. It is harass-ment, and Rabbi is just brainwashed enough to think he enjoys it," I said.

Here my father gave Rabb's fur an especially hard squeeze, which made him crawl even closer, nuzzling his head against my father's hand for more. No matter how nicely I petted

him, Rabb still inched toward my father, waiting for his rubdown and knocking his head against the nearest body part as a
reminder. I will never quite understand their relationship.

"And second," I went on, "if you don't want to pet him,
don't. I will take care of him. It is hard for you to pet him and
concentrate on your reading at the same time, anyway."

My father did not pick up on the translation (*I am jealous that my cat prefers your manhandling to my loving, gentle affection which is generally accepted by cats everywhere*), because he said
"Now you are underestimating my abilities. Do you think my
reading skills are really so poor that I can't even run my hand
over a flea-bitten rodent without being distracted?"

"He is not flea-bitten!"

"I noticed you didn't deny that he is a rodent."

Whenever I mention Rabbi to strangers, they always think
they've misheard the name. Then I have to explain: Rabbi
started out as Hansel before I got him, then became Frisbee
when my sister's friend suggested the name. But then my
father started calling him Rabbi, or the Rabb, or just Rabb.
He wrote a letter to my sister, who was doing her exchange
program in Germany at the time, explaining that the dark
patch at the bottom of Rabb's face looked like a beard, and
that Rabb always seemed to be in deep thought. My father
thought of the nickname as a high (and, in his eyes, mostly
undeserved) compliment. The name he came up with for
our other cat, Brian, however, never quite stuck. Though
the cat's irises are a distinctive and complex shade of yellow, I

just couldn't get behind the idea of calling something I loved Urine Eyes.

When I was fourteen my father announced that we had a cave cricket problem.

"A cave cricket? What is a cave cricket?"

"I don't know—your sister is the one who looked it up. She said she saw some in her room the last time she was home."

"What do they look like?"

"Big, and fast."

"But insects are our friends?"

"Not these ones. Even I think they're creepy looking. They're not dangerous, but they're still pretty nasty things. And they're not something we can look at on the porch. They're inside the house."

My father had made it clear before that although any bug could be interesting outside, even he had very little sympathy for the ones who came inside, unless it was a spider.

"We should probably call an exterminator," I said.

"I thought I'd give the cats a few days to scare them off. I saw Brian chasing one around the other day. I bet that cave cricket told his cave cricket friends."

"The boys are great hunters."

I called the cats the boys or the babies, while my father called them the miserables, or the girls, or, when feeding them, his lovely lady friends. The last two might have been flattering and even sweet, had either of the cats been female.

"Finally they have a use" was all he said.

For several nights in a row, we could hear the cats running back and forth, back and forth, through my sister's room. For some reason, the cave crickets never went past her door (or at least, not that we saw) so the cats had a safari-like opportunity: they would hunt for a few hours and then come into my room to take a nap. I never actually saw one of the crickets, but I could hear them at night. And, just a little bit louder, I could hear Brian or Rabbi calling to the other during tag-team missions or slinking quietly across the floorboards for a surprise attack. Since they both loved hunting, I would have to guess this was one of the happiest times in their lives. It made me want to cart in game for them on a regular basis, but I would have felt sorry for anything even slightly cuter than a cave cricket. Which is just about everything.

One night, the sound of a cat's running was really inter-rupting our reading. We could hear someone darting around in the room next door, having a wonderful time but making an awful lot of noise. My father tried to adjust his volume accordingly, but then the noise ended abruptly. I was listening for a moment, trying to figure out what had happened, when Rabbi suddenly appeared in my father's doorway. He was purr-ing loudly and grooming himself. He had made the kill.

When he jumped on the bed, he did not butt his head against my father. He did not drop hints that he wanted to be petted: he simply expected it to happen. I felt like a warrior's wife, greeting my husband with love as he returned from a fierce battle. I tried to avoid looking at his mouth, though, for fear of encountering dangling bug legs. The reading ended a few minutes later and my father noticed Rabbi's exuberant behavior.

"What's the deal with him?" he asked.

"Rabbi has vanquished the cave crickets," I said proudly. "Or at least a cave cricket."

"I guess if all I did was sleep all day, I'd find hunting pretty interesting too."

"Aren't you impressed, though?"

"Not particularly."

"He was defending us!"

"I doubt he thought of it that way."

"Well, at least now you can't call him a freeloader."

"I most certainly can."

I huffed off to bed, hoping Rabbi would follow. But during his proud moment, to my surprise, he chose to be with my father. As always, this annoyed me. I had to listen to my father repeat, over and over again, "You're miserable, Rabbi. You are really miserable."

I wanted to get up and defend him, to tell my father that he had killed a rather nasty bug, or two or three or four, to protect our home and defend my honor. But then I listened again, and there was one noise a little louder than my father's incessant teasing. Even from across the hall, I could hear Rabbi purring delightedly.

I tried to imagine what Rabbi thought my father was saying and decided it was *Thank you for slaying the cave crickets. You are valiant, and deserving of my love.*

And maybe in the language they alone shared, that was the correct translation after all.

CHAPTER EIGHTEEN

Day 1,948

"It's just," she said to her grandmother, "I have the feeling that I know who I am, only I'm not any more."
— Cynthia Voigt, *Dicey's Song*

My father always said that he needed time to rehearse our reading before I came up. With some of the more challenging books, especially ones with confusing dialects, I'm sure this was really the case. But he also wasn't afraid of taking the opportunity to censor the book if he thought something was inappropriate. He never wrote on the pages, that I saw, but I thought I could tell when he had substituted a word or avoided a phrase. Generally, his edits lasted less than a sentence. *Dicey's Song,* however, presented a whole new test of his improvisational skills.

I was a freshman trying to figure out fickle friends, flirty boys, and high school in general. I felt that I was supposed to do one big, dramatic gesture, that would define me and help me find my place in high school, but I couldn't figure out what. Perfecting a Norwegian accent to get the lead in the school play wasn't it. Neither was dying my hair red, blond, and back to my natural brunette in a two-year period. For a time, I thought clever T-shirts were my thing, until I realized that "Chicks Have Major Attitude" over a picture of a chicken in an army hat wasn't particularly clever, nor were any of the other shirts I owned. I went through a rather unfortunate velour pants period, but there's no need to discuss that here. Let us just agree that I was uncool, in that profoundly uncool way that only newly minted teenagers can truly perfect. Thankfully, I had no idea.

Maybe in response to my junior high endeavors, my dad and I were on a kick of reading books about young teenage girls. We went through dozens with similar plots, focusing on the trials and tribulations of those painfully self-aware years from the perspective of chipper, optimistic female narrators. I think I was supposed to learn something from them, but I never quite figured out what the message was. Even when they proclaimed absolute embarrassment, the heroines were much better at dealing with most situations. They wrote about them in their journals that night and laughed about them with their mothers a few chapters later. They sounded a lot taller than I was.

I don't remember how we found *Dicey's Song*. I know it was at a library, but I don't know what made us pick it up. My dad gave it a quick skim and decided it was for us. I didn't know enough about the plot to make an argument against or else I probably would have, just for the fun of it. Almost everything we read was my father's selection anyway—putting up the occasional protest at least reminded him that I was one half of The Streak.

"This cover makes no sense," I might say.

"It won an award," he would respond.

"The cover won an award?"

"No, the book did."

"Are you sure? It sounds like you need to get your facts straight before you decide to occupy the next month or so of our lives with this book."

"It sounds like you need a swift kick in the pants for that smart mouth."

"Yes," I would agree emphatically. "As we were both saying, I think this is a perfect book for The Streak."

Such scholarly discussions were common during the selection process, but we started *Dicey's Song* without much comment. It wasn't until we'd made a significant dent in the book that any controversy came of it.

My father went up to bed to practice the reading, as usual, while I waited at the dining room table, watching a marathon of my favorite TV show, *The Monkees*, on Nick at Nite. Once the theme song started for the third episode, I realized something was up. His usual rehearsal time was around fifteen minutes, twenty at most. When he finally called for me, I was already suspicious.

The chapter was progressing normally enough. Dicey, a girl about my age, was riding on a bus with her grandmother, and they were discussing various things going on in Dicey's life. But a few minutes in I started to guess which section had kept me waiting so long. My father started turning pages quickly, lingering for only a moment or two before flipping onward. Sometimes he barely seemed to be glancing at the text. I would have guessed he was reciting from memory, but the sentences sounded too strange. Although the dialogue just a few pages ago had been rich and complex, the conversation between Dicey and her grandmother had taken a strange turn that went something like this:

"Dicey, do you know about all the stuff?"

"Yes, Gram."

"All the stuff?"

"Of course."

"And you're ready for growing up, and whatnot?"

"Yes, I already know about that so we don't need to talk about it."

"No, we shouldn't talk about it."

"No."

"Okay then."

"Good. I'm glad we talked about it."

I looked over to see if the text was as sparse on the page as I would have imagined. No—the pages were filled and the lines of the conversation looked long. I couldn't help but wonder what I could possibly be missing. I waited for my father to finish the chapter before beginning my investigation. I didn't expect any information from him, but I tried anyway.

"That was a strange chapter, huh?"

"Yes, the dialogue was a bit confusing."

"I don't even think I understand what they were talking about."

"Who?"

He wasn't especially good at playing dumb.

"Dicey and her grandmother. The only people in the chapter. I don't think I understood what they were talking about on the bus."

"Pretty vague."

"Did you understand it?"

"No, I think they were just killing time."

I had trouble keeping a straight face.

"I bet that's exactly it."

The next day, while my dad was sorting some papers in the basement, I snuck up to his bedroom and plopped down on the floor next to his bed. He kept many of his personal books in the same pile, but our current Streak book was always on top, bookmarked and ready to go. I left the bookmark in, so that there was no chance of accidentally replacing it in a different spot and incriminating myself. I didn't like keeping secrets, but as long as we were both being secretive, I was determined to be little better at it.

I opened to the chapter from the night before and began reading backward. There was the now-infamous conversation between Dicey and her grandmother, but it was not quite how he had represented it. It was about puberty, which hadn't been at all clear in the edited version. Gram uncomfortably brought up menstruation and boys to Dicey; and Dicey, also uncomfortable but not quite as much, agreed to come to her with any questions. It was quirky, and realistic, and not at all graphic. Actually, it was a rather classy way for a parent to approach these subjects. I could envision someone, someone other than my father, giving this book to a daughter to help get those conversations started in real life. When I found another skipped passage, about Gram taking Dicey to purchase her first bra, I had to put down the book because I couldn't see the pages through my tears.

I was laughing uncontrollably, squirming around on my father's rough bedroom carpet until I had rug burn up and down my arms (my velour pants, of course, protected my legs). The tears were streaming down my face so quickly that I almost wanted to look in a mirror and make sure none of my freckles had washed off. My stomach hurt in that wonderful, out-of-breath way that is somehow exactly like doing crunches, but opposite.

My father had gone to an extreme effort to cut out the exact conversations that we should have been having. He could have taken the easy way out, giving me the information through Gram instead of broaching it himself. I'm sure this is what most single fathers would have done. Instead, though, he went to painstaking, exhausting efforts to mask the nature of the conversation and, indirectly, the plot of the entire novel. For some reason, it struck me as the silliest thing he had ever done. I imagined what our conversation on the bus might have been if we were living out *Alice's Song*, and I realized it might be strikingly similar to my dad's improvisation the night before. It would just require a role reversal.

"Dad," I would say, "do you want to talk about the stuff?"

"No, I think you know about the stuff."

"All the stuff?"

"Yes," he would say. "You know about all the stuff."

"Okay, so we shouldn't talk about it?"

"No, we definitely shouldn't talk about it."

I kept replaying this scene in my head. Realistically, we would never even have a conversation of *that* depth. I think he was telling himself that I wasn't quite ready to talk, and that *Dicey's Song* raised questions I didn't even have yet. But really, he wasn't ready to talk, and he never would be. We never had a big discussion on the topic. Once, he told me that he hoped I wasn't "jiving" and that I shouldn't give into societal pressures. I thought we were having a meaningful conversation about relationships, or maybe drugs, until I figured out that he was telling me not to spend any money on him for Father's Day. I have never heard *jiving* used in that context again.

I sat on the floor, skimming other books from The Streak and looking for my father's omissions. I felt sort of sorry for him, realizing how uncomfortable he was. More noticeably, though, I felt my throat getting tighter. Through the laughter, I had to remind myself to breathe.

CHAPTER NINETEEN

Day 2,015

Do what you can to make it good. And remember, as we used to say, that life is like a pudding: it takes both the salt and the sugar to make a really good one.

—Joan W. Blos, *A Gathering of Days*

There's a big gray spider setting up shop in my room! Come see!"

I heard a low grumbling noise from my father's room, followed by some raspy coughing.

"Hurry up! She's going to crawl back into the windowsill! She has a little nook in there."

Again the strange noise, like someone playing a clarinet without using any of the keys.

"What are you doing? You're missing it!" I yelled, poking my head into his bedroom.

He looked greenish and pale. His face was covered in sweat. I could see through his white shirt.

"Oh my goodness, what happened to you?" I ran up to the bed and tried to put my hand on my father's forehead, but he batted it away and wrinkled his eyebrows together to show his frustration.

"Hhhhhh," he said, moving his lips as though he was saying more than that. I laughed. Then I realized he actually *was* saying more than that. I came closer and leaned over him, ear first.

"I think I might be coming down with something," my father whispered. His voice was thin and choppy, like someone had been running it over a cheese grater. His breath was abnormally warm.

"I'll take it a step further for you—you are sick," I corrected him, imitating his voice to bring attention to just how awful he sounded.

"I'm not sick," he wheezed. "I never get sick. I've never been sick a day in my life. But I'm a little under the weather. I'm just running in a lower gear right now." He coughed a few more times.

"Things running in this gear usually don't work. Things running in this gear are broken."

"I guess I should go see the doctor pretty soon," he said. He rubbed sweat off with his hand.

"How soon is pretty soon? Today? In an hour? Should I call and see what she has open?"

"Geezle peezle, Lovie, I've got enough vigor left in me to make a phone call."

"Yes, but they'll hang up once they decide that they've got a prank caller doing a Donald Duck impression. Are you sure you don't want me to call for you? I've got nothing better to do."

"Rrrrhhhhhhhsh," he said, bracing himself to get out of bed.

"What was that? Yes?"

"I'll do it," he whispered. "They're doctors. They're used to situations like this."

As it turned out, he was right. They were used to situations like this: they'd seen their share of sore throats and stubborn old men. When my father came home he swore they'd told him to take a few cold pills and get on with his regular schedule, but I imagined rest had also come up, though he failed to mention it. It seemed that his only real problem was his throat, which was raw and red. I could see it when he talked, maybe because I had to get so close to hear what he was actually saying.

"That looks like it's killing you. Did they tell you to gargle with salt water? That's the worst."

"It actually doesn't feel as bad as it sounds. I feel pretty much normal at this point, I just haven't gotten my voice back. These words aren't even coming from my throat right now."

He showed me how he was puffing air up in his cheeks and mouthing the words as he released it, creating a sound that vaguely resembled talking but was more closely related to whistling.

"That's all you're doing? No wonder I can't understand a word you're saying. Just talk from your throat if you say it really doesn't hurt. Did the doctor tell you to rest it or something?"

"No, it just doesn't work. Nothing comes out. There's no sound. Like someone turned it off."

"Weird! That is actually kind of creepy. You are like some sort of voiceless alien. Cool."

"Well," he whistle-whispered, "it's got me a little worried, to tell you the truth."

"Oh, that is cute of you! I didn't think you were ever concerned about your health. I'm glad you are. But don't worry at all. The doctor just saw you; she would have told you if something was up."

"No," he said, "it's not that. I feel fine and this should pass in a couple of days. I'm worried about"— he leaned closer and mouthed both syllables painstakingly— "*The Streak.*"

I listened without understanding for a minute or two, just nodding and smiling at my father's sick ramblings. But then what he'd said sunk in, and suddenly I was worried, too. Why hadn't this occurred to me from the moment I heard his voice, or lack thereof, earlier that morning? It only made sense, of course, that he was worried: his whole job during The Streak was using his voice. There wasn't too much else to it. His voice had never been a problem before; my father, as he claimed, never actually gets sick. He wasn't even sick-sick now, since he was already feeling and looking better. The only issue was his throat, and for such a small tube, that was a surprisingly big problem. I started to feel a little sick myself as I wondered what would become of our tradition.

We had to take control of the situation. We both spent the day pondering solutions. I asked, if he read me a picture book with big words, could he mouth the sentences while I also read them to myself? No, he decided, that was cheating. Really, that was me reading to myself while he chaperoned. He thought of reading something we both knew by heart and that maybe rhymed, like a Poe poem, where I'd know what he was saying even if I couldn't really hear it. But if my idea didn't work, his didn't, either: it wasn't really reading if we both had it memorized. It was synchronized recitation, and it was unacceptable. Whenever my father got a new idea he'd jot it down on a notepad and leave it by my chair at the dining room table, but by the end of the day none of our ideas seemed any more logical than the first few. All of them, we decided, weren't quite up to the standards we had set for The Streak. Now my concern was starting to feel like panic.

I took my cats out on the porch for some supervised playtime. This was their favorite part of any day, and a good part of mine because it gave me a chance to think. As I sat on the porch steps, drawing with a pebble I'd found that had a chalk-like consistency, I found myself doodling "The Streak" over and over again. Sometimes it was in cursive, with big, loopy letters, sometimes in all capital letters, declarative and assuring, but mostly in my tiny, neat print. After all these years—I was now fifteen—I tried to picture what it might feel like if The Streak had to end tonight. I knew it wouldn't—if The Streak ever ended suddenly, it would be because one of us couldn't make it home. If we were both in the same place at the same time, as we were right now and would be later in the evening,

The Streak would go on. We would figure something out. But there was a part of me that wondered about things, like falling out of the window of a car or accidentally ingesting enough toothpaste to warrant calling the poison control number on the back of the tube. And that part couldn't help picturing what it might feel like to end The Streak tonight. We'd pick up the book, and my father would attempt to read, but the sounds just wouldn't come out. He'd get a few words out, but then his whisper would become totally inaudible, and we'd have to stop. After all, he wasn't really reading to me if I couldn't understand him. We'd sit in silence and know, just know, that it was the last night and there was nothing we could do about it. It would be sad, maybe the saddest thing that had ever happened to me. Certainly the saddest thing that had ever happened to my father, I thought. More than anything, to him, it would mean defeat. I knew he wouldn't let it happen.

I took the pebble I'd been doodling with and underlined the words: THE STREAK. I wrote them bigger, with confidence. We'd figure something out. We had to.

Our decision was ultimately to do whatever we deemed closest to our regular routine, and we decided that was reading as usual, but at a close range. A very close range.

"Ghhhhjhhh," my father said, as he sat down on the couch. We'd relocated from his bed to the couch so I could sit up next to him and get a better spot, right next to his mouth, leaning in as close as I could.

"I would tell you that you have to speak up, but I guess that wouldn't be very funny, huh?"

"Come closer," I watched his lips say. His throat sounded even weaker than it had earlier.

I leaned onto him just as he started a coughing fit, causing me to jump back immediately. He continued coughing for quite some time, long enough to give me a chance to run upstairs and get hand sanitizer. I put it on his hands, and then my hands, and then my face. It made my cheeks cold and dry, but I felt a bit safer all the same. When I took my position back, it was with cautious deliberation.

"Can you understand me?" I finally realized he was saying. My ear was so close to his lips that I could hear the spit forming in his mouth between words. My father, who still hates physical closeness at any time, had probably not let anyone this near him since I was a toddler, or maybe since he and my mother were still happily married. I realized, feeling sorry for the both of them, that I didn't know which of those events came first. Not wanting to offend him, I tried to keep any part of my body from touching him.

"When we last left off," he began, once I had stopped squirming around.

He always gave me a reminder of the chapter from the previous night before delving into a new one. Although *Maniac Magee*, the story of an athletic orphan searching for a home, wasn't particularly hard to follow, tonight I was really grateful for the help. Otherwise, the only thing I could really focus on was the strangeness of the situation. I imagined what the caption might read if someone snapped a photo of us right then and put it in the newspaper, like the photos of the kids playing by fire hydrants they sometimes stuck next to the weather forecast on a really hot day. It might be something like:

James Brozina, age 55, reads to his daughter, 15. Due to some recent medical issues, Brozina was unavailable for a quote. No one can explain why his face looks so greenish, or why his daughter is sitting so close to him. A reader from Vineland points out that they are not actually touching in any way. Further investigation into this matter forthcoming.

I brought my attention back to the moment long enough, though, to realize that my father was actually doing a superb job. The deep bass he had created for Earl, the zoo groundskeeper, was brought up an octave, and the girlish singsong of bibliophile Amanda Beale was brought down, but the words were rolling off his tongue in a beautiful, hypnotic way. He said them with certainty, closing his mouth firmly after each sentence, taking a breath and starting anew. It was obvious that he had to put in a great deal of effort to reach this quality. His face was sweating, and this time it wasn't from the fever. He strained, occasionally trying to switch back to his throat but quickly realizing that there was no sound left in the pipe. So the whisper became more comfortable, and he used facial expressions to supplement it. He wasn't so hard to understand at all. He made it look easy, like always. There was no question that he had rehearsed the chapter many, many times since realizing he was sick.

For the next three days, his voice was shot. He practiced each of those nights for an hour, maybe more, the few short pages he had to read to keep The Streak alive by our high standards. When his voice came back in full by the end of that week, I couldn't completely convince myself that it was any better than his recent work. Undoubtedly, he was happy to be back to his old self, reading at what he perceived to be his highest level of quality.

But I remember that summer a little differently than he might. It was hot, very hot, from June to September. The fireflies came out earlier than ever and sometimes stayed late into the evening. Someone down the street from us got an outdoor fireplace, and the whole street smelled like wood chips and smoke for months. And there was something else. A sense of joy, a sense of pride, that we'd overcome another obstacle. Nothing at all could stand in our way at this point. We were meeting the challenges The Streak threw at us with ease. We were fearless and invincible. And his hollow whisper sounding out a children's book was more beautiful than the most robust rendition of Shakespeare.

CHAPTER TWENTY

Day 2,340

"It's really dreadful," she muttered to herself, "the way all the creatures argue. It's enough to drive one crazy!"
—Lewis Carroll, *Alice's Adventures in Wonderland*

It was one of those hot, humid days when you stuck to anything you touched as though you were made of maple syrup. Right now I was stuck to the car seat, heading to Pennsylvania with my dad and sister to visit a museum and a couple of public gardens. My father was absolutely opposed to turning on the air conditioner at home until July, so the opportunity to ride around with the windows down should have excited me as much as it would have excited any floppy-eared dog. But thirty or so miles into the trip, with the sunlight pouring in relentlessly through my side of the car, I was feeling less than enthusiastic about the experience. My body felt swollen from the heat, a sausage tightly packed and about to burst from its casing. I reached to pat my sister, who was home for a bit before starting her first adult, full-time job. She still rode in the backseat with me, and I wanted to thank her for the visit with a pat on the knee. It seemed like too much effort, though, so I just wiggled my fingers at her while humming in her general direction. She was reading a book about antiques and pleading with my father to turn down or turn off Elvis, so she misconstrued my friendly gesture as an attempt to tickle her and slapped my hand. We were off to a great start.

The one great comfort to me in my sweaty state was Hank's Place. Appearing like a mirage in the distance, Hank's sang to me sweetly from beside the highway, offering hearty split pea soup and egg-and-cheese sandwiches all day. It was the quintessential greasy spoon, with the slogan "Where hungry people eat and friendly people meet!" as though there were no alternatives for either. Hank's made any trip, even a hot and sticky one, worthwhile. If my family was traveling through the area, it was a guaranteed stop. I had even skipped breakfast in preparation for my feast.

Our car rolled on past the parking lot, and I jumped up immediately, straining the seat belt and pointing like a hunting dog.

"I want to get to the Brandywine Museum before the crowds start," my dad said.

"But I haven't eaten yet!"

"And whose bright idea was that?"

"I had a bowl of oatmeal, but I could eat. As long as we double back in an hour or two, we might all have bigger appetites," Kath offered.

She was attempting to be a nonpartisan, logical peace-maker. There is nothing more annoying in a heated argument than a nonpartisan, logical peacemaker. I swatted at her. My father kept driving.

"Thanks a lot," I hissed, as I slumped down in my protesting rag doll position.

"No problem," she said sincerely, and returned to her book.

When we arrived at the museum, I was determined to leave and get back to the food as quickly as I could.

"There's a new exhibit on ducks this week," the woman at the desk mentioned cheerfully, as she handed us our admission buttons, "and tours are available every twenty minutes." She was speaking softly, and no else seemed to have heard her.

"No, thank you," I responded in a sympathetic whisper, turning my back to my family and barely moving my lips. "My sister is horribly afraid of ducks."

The woman looked at Kath, put her hand over her heart, and nodded.

Finally we were ready to go, bracing ourselves for the weight of the heat as we pushed open the glass doors. We'd managed to keep our circuit to less than half an hour in total, and I was feeling generous. I suggested a stroll through the gardens before brunch.

"Brunch?"my father said. "I thought we were just getting pastries at one of the gardens."

"Oooh," Kath agreed, "I could go for some chocolate cake."

"No no no, we made plans to go to Hank's."

The sun was making me dizzy, and the thought of eating something heavy and sweet set my stomach swaying. More importantly, though, I had a blood sugar problem and could not eat something sweet as a meal. I verbalized my concern.

"Little Orphan Egg," my sister said, using her nickname for me and giggling.

"Your life is a Shakespearean tragedy," my father added, getting in on the act.

The heat was really getting to me, but their teasing was worse. In a childish moment of confusion and resentment, I darted off into a corner of the garden and crouched behind a statue of a pig. It was made of bronze and burned my arm.

"*What happens to a dream deferred?*" I wrote frantically in a notebook I had pulled out of my bag, quoting Langston Hughes and trying to be philosophical at sixteen years old. I couldn't think what he would say about not being able to go to your favorite restaurant, so I drew a picture of my foot. In an angry sort of way.

I could see them peeking at me and trying not to smile.

"It's not funny!" I finally called out.

"You can't get a fried egg, so you are hiding behind a statue of a pig and writing in your journal," my sister pointed out.

"*I am not writing in my journal! I am reflecting in my reflecting notebook!*"

They couldn't keep straight faces anymore.

"Could you reflect at the next stop, maybe over a cookie?" my father asked, laughing.

I huffed out and didn't say a word. When we stopped at

the garden's cafeteria, I used my own money to get a sandwich and refused to even look at the desserts.

About an hour later I was feeling social again and talking to my sister, though I hadn't quite forgiven her treason yet.

"Why did you bring a textbook?" I asked her, pointing at the heavy reference book on antiques that she had pulled out again as we headed to our final stop.

"I am taking a class on early American furniture," she explained, "and I want to be prepared to fully enjoy the house tour we are taking at the Winterthur Estate."

"Like fun we are taking that tour!" my father interrupted. "It was about time for my nap two hours ago! We're going to go for a loop on the turnip truck and beat it back home in jig time."

The garden tram was the "turnip truck," a term he insisted on using in front of the museum curators and tour guides. Luckily, they were always too confused to be offended.

Kath looked as though someone had just informed her she'd been injected with a slow, lethal poison. Her face got white, her eyes got big, and she reached for my hand.

"We...aren't...going on the tour? That's the whole reason I came home for the weekend!"

"I thought you came home because you loved me," I said.

"No," she explained.

I considered for a moment before weighing in.

"We've done that tour a million times. If we're going to do anything extra, it should be a stop at Hank's. And that's not even extra, since it should have happened earlier anyway."

"What would you do," my father began, "if someone said that you could eat out for free at any chain restaurant for the rest of your life, but you had to sleep in a coffin every night instead of a bed?"

His infamous scenario questions were a sure indicator that he was listening to neither of us. Kath looked at me for support, but I was reminded of my dark moments just hours ago, pining for soup in the shadow of a pig statue. She had not come to my rescue. I shook my head and stared out the window. My sister curled herself up against the car door and began to sulk. She looked at us with moody eyes and pursed lips. She reminded me of Rabbi, when you stopped petting him without warning. And because she had not fought in my defense earlier, I did not feel a bit sorry for her.

Twenty minutes later, I was feeling very sorry for her.

"I'm sorry you didn't get to see the boring chairs," I said in a soothing tone.

She looked at me suspiciously from her corner, like a snake who was trying to decide if she should strike or just go to sleep until I went away.

"I'm sorry you didn't get to stuff yourself like a turkey at Dad's expense," she finally relented.

To make ourselves feel better, we played Tales of Fang. It was a game we invented when we inherited my grandmother's cat, who had once been called Miss Kitty but was appropriately renamed Granny Fang because of her old age and penchant for biting. She absolutely oozed hatred like no other creature before or since. To play the game, you need only think of a scenario and explain how Granny Fang might wreck it. Usually, her method involved her trademark fang.

"Okay, let's say your boyfriend was about to propose."

"Too easy," my sister said. "Granny Fang would bite my finger off so that I had nowhere to put the ring."

"What about your wedding day?"

"Even more obvious—she'd stick her fang in just enough places to get blood all over my dress."

"You make it sound like bullfighting."

"Yes, only more violent."

We started laughing until my father yelled from the front seat,

"Cut that out! What did you say about me?"

We looked at each other.

"Nothing. We were talking about Granny Fang."

"Who called me an old bull?"

"One," my sister said, "that is not even a real insult. And two, no one said that."

My father kept his eyes on the road but his face was getting red.

"I don't like you girls whispering back there."

"We are talking at a normal volume!"

"Remember that you are mostly deaf, Dad."

He reached for the glove compartment.

"If you're not going to include everyone, you're not going to talk in my car," he said, pulling out an Elvis CD. He pushed Play and turned up the volume, and we drove the rest of the way home without speaking another word.

When we got home, my father read to me from a book that ended up being one of my favorites from The Streak— *Surviving the Applewhites*, by Stephanie S. Tolan. I initially liked it because the characters were putting on a production of *The Sound of Music*, and at the time, musicals were a big part of my life. It was the first book we'd ever read that was about theater, and I felt a special connection. But tonight the connection ran deeper, as I considered the Applewhite family for what they were: eight very different people who seemed to, for the most part, get along quite well living under one roof. They squeezed themselves, and even a visitor, into their house and still enjoyed life completely. A family of eight! I couldn't imagine it. Whenever Kath came home, we became three, and we couldn't even handle that. The house felt tight and cramped, and we couldn't quite figure out how to fit all of us in. I wished we could, but we were no Applewhites.

Today was just another example, and I didn't know whether to laugh or cry, because it always happened something like this: I would get mad but back down when Kath got cranky, and she would just be coming around when my dad lost his temper. We didn't want to admit it, but we had adjusted to life apart. Just being together meant that someone would feel attacked, or ganged up on, no matter what we were doing. We could last for Christmas, or maybe a long weekend. But most of the time, we couldn't figure out our group dynamic because even if we got it right once, my sister would be on her way again and we'd have to make a fresh start at the next visit. We all felt guilty, but there seemed to be nothing we could do to fix it. Apologies didn't make much of a difference when everyone was miserable. And there weren't even enough of us to put on a production of *The Sound of Music* the way the Applewhites did.

That night, after my father closed the book, I stood in my sister's doorway as she finished her own evening routine of praying beside her bed.

"What do you think Granny Fang would do if she was the host of your visit?" I asked.

Kath got into bed, pulled up her covers, and turned out her light.

"She'd probably just put us all in the same room. That would be her most cruel trick."

I headed back to my room and sat on the edge of my bed, hugging my legs to my chest.

"This will get better," I told my knees reassuringly.

CHAPTER TWENTY-ONE

Day 2,578

*Something...gave me permission to do things I had never
done before. Never even thought of doing. Something there
triggered the unfolding of those parts that had been incubat-
ing. Things that had lain inside me, curled up like the turtle
hatchlings newly emerged from their eggs, taking time in the
dark of their nest to unfurl themselves.*
—E. L. Konigsburg, *The View from Saturday*

My full name is Kristen Alice Ozma Brozina.

Names are funny things. Parents spend months,
sometimes years discussing them and weighing options, often
deciding on one before you're even an air-breathing creature. Or they wait until you come out, all pink and puffy and
maybe bald, to realize that somehow, they can just tell, you
are a Ryan or a Jimmy or a Shana. Or a Kristen.

I was not always supposed to be Kristen. At first, I was a JJ.
My mother's ultrasound showed clearly, beyond the shadow
of a doubt, that I was a boy—which was a pretty clever trick,
if you ask me. So when I came out without all the match-
ing parts to be James Junior, my mom decided on Kristen

right then and there because one of her former students had the name, and the girl was apparently very nice. It was a last-minute name, and I could sense, even then I'm sure, that it was not right for me.

Many people say that the world was not ready for them, but in my case it is a literal fact. After stripping my father of his "the First" title before he even got to use it, my parents took me home and moved me into the Phil Collins room.

"What does one do in a Phil Collins room?" a friend recently asked me.

"Appreciate Phil Collins."

"Do you need an entire room to do that?"

"No. You need half a room. You can keep a baby in the other half."

There were pictures, and records, and posters, all mixed in with the yellow and blue baby decorations. One poster in particular sticks out in my mind, because it somehow kept its place on my door for years after the rest of the memorabilia was gone. It advertised the Genesis Invisible Tour, which I always found confusing.

"Really," I told my mother one night, as I was putting on my pajamas, "that concert was probably a waste of money. I don't think they were ever even there. I don't know if a person can be invisible, probably yes, but I don't think a whole band can, or at least not at one time. I hope the tickets were at least cheap."

So I lived in the Phil Collins room, and my name was Kristen because it could not be James, and all along I knew this was wrong. But it took me sixteen years to change either.

When I was a sophomore in high school, I decided that

my room needed a makeover. It had always been a mess, but I realized that maybe, really, this was because I didn't feel like it was my own. So I took down all the old posters and replaced them with photos of my friends, rolled up the carpet and invested in floor polish. I cleaned, and decorated, and realized that when the space felt like it was meant not for Phil Collins, or JJ, but me, I actually wanted to keep it tidy. Parents, take note: maybe a coat of bright purple paint or a few heavy metal posters aren't such a bad idea after all.

And as long as I was reclaiming things, I figured that my name might as well be one of them. So gradually, I started letting people know that I didn't want to be called Kristen.

"What do you want me to call you?" people would always ask.

"Well, anything, I guess. But not Kristen."

It felt weird saying it, even if I had always been thinking it. But because I never told anyone anything specific, I got a hodgepodge of names. What I really wanted people to call me, though, was Alice Ozma.

Alice. Ozma. Alice, and then, Ozma. They sounded perfect together, like two names meant to follow each other, but even better; Billie Jean, Cindy Lou, Sara Jane—take cover. I loved hearing the sounds back to back, the way they rolled off my tongue and stayed in the air, hanging there for just a second like hot breath on a cold day. Alice, a perfectly American, wholesome, calm name was followed surprisingly by Ozma, a dark-haired exotic gem that usually led to questions. They were questions that I loved to answer.

My parents made a deal that my mother could pick the first

names of girls and my father could pick the middle names, and vice versa, so Alice and Ozma are his doing. They are names appropriate for the daughter of The Streak, though I wasn't that girl yet when he picked them. My father wanted to name me after strong females in literature. Luckily, he already had some experience reading with my sister and had two specific young ladies in mind.

Alice, from Lewis Carroll's *Alice's Adventures in Wonderland*, is full of questions and content to admit that she doesn't always know the answers. She considers, and ponders, and of course, makes mistakes. She was a logical choice for a middle name. But when my father thought of Ozma, a heroine in every book in L. Frank Baum's Oz series except the first (and most well-known), he was torn. Ozma is the intelligent, unwaveringly fair ruler of the Land of Oz who befriends and guides Dorothy. She is logical, and kind, and loyal. And my father was left with quite a decision to make.

So rather than choosing one, he put them back to back and liked how they sounded. Alice Ozma. Naturally. That is who I became.

These were the names I loved the most. I doodled them in notebooks and made a point of signing everything with my full, legal name in an effort to include them. When people asked what they meant, I enjoyed telling the story, every single time, no matter how often it came up. When people *guessed* what they meant, I knew I had found an instant friend.

At sixteen, when I started cautiously, nervously, asking people to come up with something, anything but Kristen, many people were stumped. To those, I suggested Alice Ozma.

"It is very literary," I would say, feeling like a boardwalk pitchman, "but with an earthy undertone. It sounds like summer rain, or maybe jasmine. When you say it together, it is the most logical thing in the world."

And when they still resisted, I would say, "Well, you can at least try it."

But I wanted to encourage the effort. One of my teachers once mused that finding your place in high school is all about selling your brand, so I started selling Alice Ozma every chance I got. I had an Alice Ozma blog, and an Alice Ozma screen name for chatting with my friends online, and an Alice Ozma e-mail address. I tried signing notes as Alice Ozma. When I started taking art lessons I scribbled simply "Ozma" in the corner of my paintings to save room, but it looked lonesome. They needed to come together, as a pairing, or maybe a balancing act.

Eventually, most people stopped calling me Kristen, but to my dismay Alice Ozma never really caught on. Only here and there, with some people, in certain circles, on certain occasions.

"Why won't anyone call me what I want to be called?" I asked my father one night after our reading. "I mean, it is my *name*. I didn't make it up."

"They are just jealous. It's eating them alive, because their parents picked their names out of baby books."

He rested his head in his hands, always proud to talk about his parenting skills.

"Do you think it is something I have to grow into? Like long hair?"

I hadn't cut my hair in a year, and though the length

seemed appropriate, it didn't look quite right on my head. He wrinkled his eyebrows and made a face like he was blowing out a candle.

"Are you serious about this hair thing? You look like a swamp creature."

It was lucky that I had decent self-esteem.

"Or do you remember the movie *Attack of the Killer Shrews*, where they used dogs with carpets on their backs as the monsters? That is sort of what it looks like."

Yes, that self-esteem really came in handy.

I didn't think people were jealous, as he suggested. If anything, some people thought the names, and the stories behind them, were a bit nerdy. Those were people who probably would not have appreciated The Streak. So in some crowds I kept my name preferences, and my reading experiences, to myself.

Every once in a while, though, when I made my request and told my story, I'd see a flicker. The new friend's eyes would light up.

"Really?" she would say. "Is that true? Does your school ID say that?"

I would show her.

"Wow, that is kind of neat. I mean it's really neat. It's different. So is your dad, like, really into books? Did he read to you a lot when you were a kid?"

I was sixteen and, like any sixteen-year-old, unsure what people might think if they knew more about me, or about my family. But if they were really interested in my middle names, and asked questions, and smiled at all the right times, I knew I was safe. That was the best moment of all, because there was something I was waiting to tell anyone who wouldn't laugh.

"Well," I would begin, "does your family have any... traditions?"

CHAPTER TWENTY-TWO

Day 2,740

So just think: you have nothing more to fear for the rest of your life. Even if you put your pants on backwards or wear two different-colored socks, a hat with grapes on it, and a diaper, you will never look as stupid as you did a moment ago. Obviously you will never be embarrassed again.
    —Stephen Manes, *Be a Perfect Person in Just Three Days*

The thing about community theatre is, it takes time. Every hobby takes time, that is obvious. But in theatre you don't often make your own schedule, and therein lies the problem for a Streak daughter.

When I first got involved in theatre, there wasn't a Streak. At age four, I gladly helped out a local high school that was looking for a child for a bit part in their spring musical. I enjoyed the experience immensely and went on to perform in many productions without worrying too much about the time they took up or the late-night rehearsals. When The Streak began, though, those long nights became an issue.

It was a brilliantly clear, absolutely perfect fall evening.

It should have been winter, but for some reason, it wasn't. Not quite yet. The leaves were still hanging on with all their might, dancing in the breeze and showing their reds and golds defiantly to the slowly creeping frosts. You couldn't see your breath, but you might need a sweater if you were going to be outside for long after dark. It was, in my opinion, the perfect sort of weather for many things: buying pumpkin-flavored fudge, or making ice cream sandwiches using ginger snaps, or sitting on the front porch with a glass of cider, hoping to catch the glorious scent of someone burning leaves. Because fall is my favorite season, I would say it was the perfect weather for just about anything. But it was by no means, not even in the slightest bit, good weather for total embarrassment. I'm not sure what that weather is. Probably snow or rain or any other condition that creates limited visibility.

I was at a rehearsal for a production of a somewhat obscure, antiquated musical about family values and American ideals. Actually, the rehearsal itself had ended almost an hour ago. We were now going through the tedious process of "notes." In theatre, notes are just about anything the director, musical director, choreographer, costume designer, technical crew, or general assembled party notices about the production, good or bad. For a five-minute scene, notes can easily last fifteen to twenty minutes. I once had a thirty-second nonspeaking role in a production and got over five minutes of notes, ranging from my posture to the angle of my hat. Notes can be a long process.

I was pulled into the chorus for this particular show at the last minute when the director realized none of their sopranos were actually high sopranos. My job was to sing high notes, and walk across the stage in a shawl, and hand a book to one of the main characters at one point. I did not have lines or any solos, which worked well with my busy schedule. But since my job was basically to blend in to the crowd, I always wished I could skip notes.

I was sitting on the edge of the stage, dangling my legs over and looking at the clock. For the past hour or so, it seemed to be moving at lightning speed. Just a minute ago, I was picking at a hole near the ankle of my pantyhose and the clock clearly said 10:45. Now the hole was only slightly larger, and the skin under it only a little irritated from my rubbing, and it appeared to be 11:30. I held my head in my hands and tried to keep from shifting my weight in an effort to seem perfectly calm. If anyone had been looking at me specifically, they might have guessed I was tired and eager to go home and get to bed. Which would have been very reasonable for someone who had school the next day.

In actuality, though, I was crossing my fingers and hoping against hope that my father was not about to walk through the door. I didn't have a cell phone yet, but I told him I would borrow someone else's and call him when rehearsal was about to end so he could leave to pick me up. I had planned to call him when we got to the notes for the second act, but we were less than halfway through the first act, and I knew he was panicking, worrying that we weren't going to have time to get our reading in before midnight. If he wasn't driving over right now, it was because he was already parked outside, practicing the reading by flashlight and occasionally lifting the beam to check his watch and nervously walk over to look through a window.

I could picture this all so clearly because similar things had happened before. Rehearsals went late, and my father would show up, book in hand, and gesture to me from the back of the auditorium. But generally, a theatre is a busy place and there is enough commotion that one white-haired man standing in the shadows could easily be overlooked.

In these situations, I would gesture to him and try to communicate that he could wait outside if he wanted and I would meet him as soon as I had a break in my scenes. Even a lead is generally offstage for a decent amount of time, so I'd run out to the parking lot, sit on the hood of the car or lean against the building, and listen for ten or so minutes before running back inside. If I missed a cue, I usually just made a general excuse like "I'm sorry, I had to step outside." The Streak could be embarrassing in the right (or wrong) context, but more than anything, it was hard to explain. When I did explain, I always had to give the full story, since "I'm sorry, my dad had to read me a few pages of Sherlock Holmes before midnight" generally just added to the confusion.

My concern, in this particular situation, was that there was no dark corner for him to quietly wait in and signal to me from. We were rehearsing in a rather small room because the group was in the process of looking for a new theater, and the space was tight, cramped, and bright. The entire cast could barely fit on the makeshift stage at one time, so some had spilled into chairs scattered around the room. The director himself (and a few rather nice-looking teenage boys) were seated directly in front of the door to the parking lot, and every light in the room was on.

I started picking at the hole in my pantyhose even more. I tried to make a plan. If I asked to leave, I wouldn't be allowed—someone else had just tried it and the director insisted that if he had to stay, we had to stay. I could head toward the bathroom and see if there was a door in that back hallway, but I'd run the risk of being out of sight when my father came in, which would get him even more worried. I thought of saying that I was going to get something from my car, but since I was always trying to bum a ride, everyone in the cast was well aware that I could not drive. I could say that my father was waiting in the parking lot to tell me something, but I'd be accused of checking a cell phone during notes— otherwise, how would I know he was out there?—and that was strictly forbidden.

I felt as though I was going to fall through the stage. I can't say what was so terrifying about the thought of my father coming into rehearsal. I think mostly, it was the fact that I had no idea what he would say or do. Any number of things could happen, and only about 20 percent of them weren't particularly embarrassing. I think the root of embarrassment is feeling totally misunderstood, wanting to explain yourself over and over but knowing that you won't make much sense to anyone even if you do. The Streak always posed that sort of problem. No one would understand; therefore, it was at least a little embarrassing. Interesting, and a great conversation starter when talking to someone who might understand, yes. But at sixteen, when feeling misunderstood is about as standard as sprouting pimples and thinking you're the first person to truly *get* the Beatles, The Streak could also be difficult. Sometimes I wasn't proud of it. I wish I could say otherwise.

I sat and pictured the door opening so many times that when it finally did, I didn't react at first. I couldn't quite connect that this time I wasn't imagining it. My dad walked in and looked around, but somehow failed to notice when I eventually began waving from the stage. The bright lights can be blinding, especially when you're walking in from the dark. He covered his eyes and squinted, rotating in a little circle, until the director finally said, sounding a bit annoyed, "Can I help you?"

"I need to speak with my daughter" was all my dad said for the time being, and I breathed a sigh of relief that he used the word *speak* instead of *read*. Then I pulled my breath back in and held it, wondering what the director would say. He was a very nice man, fatherly and warm, but the rehearsal had gone poorly and it was wearing on his patience.

"I'm sorry," he said. "I understand that it is late and I apologize for keeping her. But these are important notes that I think she will want to hear. We should be done in twenty minutes or less, if you'd like to take a seat."

My father's entrance was holding up the end of an already seven-hour rehearsal, and people started whispering. They were trying to figure out who he was, and though I wouldn't have minded letting them know, there was no way of informing the whole crowd without standing up on the stage and announcing it. I waved again, but my father wasn't even looking toward the stage.

"Well," my father said briskly, "that's not gonna fly. It needs to be right now."

I suddenly got an idea, simple but clear and effective—my father need only say, "It's urgent," and there would be no question of letting me go, at least for a few minutes. It was vague but earnest. People would assume there had been a death in the family. They would feel sorry for us as we headed toward the exit, instead of staring at my father with contempt as they were now. I closed my eyes and tried to send the message to him telepathically, but my skills weren't as sharp as they should have been because that's not what he said. What he said, in a low voice that he clearly intended to be a whisper, was: "I need to read to her by midnight."

As I constantly remind him during concerts and lectures, my father has yet to learn what an actual whisper sounds like. His version actually made the situation a little worse, because he was perfectly audible but added a somewhat conspiratorial tone to his voice. Then he finally saw me and pointed. I don't know how he was able to find me, since I was slumped over like a rag doll and trying to bury myself in the folds of my dress. Maybe my red face attracted his attention.

Heads turned. I could practically hear the eyebrows rising.

"What?" the director asked, staring up at him and obviously assuming he'd misheard.

My father just nodded and pointed at me again. I flashed a weak smile and hoped that the heat coming off my face would set off the fire alarm and give me an excuse to run out the back door. Someone near me whispered, "Let her go. I'm not going to sit here all night."

There was a general mumbling of agreement, which the director may have heard because, after looking at my father for another moment or two, he said, "Well, all right, then."

My father waited at the door as I made my way down the stairs and toward him, hearing people ask from all around me, "What did he say he has to do? Read her what?"

Someone close to my age pulled on my hem as I walked by and asked, "Is this some sort of a religious thing?"

I eventually made it to the door. Before I left, as was customary, I hugged and kissed the director good-bye. He looked confused but smiled at my father over my shoulder, apparently trying to convince him that all was well. Just as the door shut behind me, I could hear him announce, "Well, no one *else* is getting out of here until notes are done!"

Because we couldn't make it home before midnight, we read a chapter of *Ten Little Indians* by Agatha Christie in the parking lot, leaning up against the car. My father held his flashlight over the pages, despite the fact that it was quite easy to see by the streetlights. As we were finishing, the cast began trickling out to their cars. Most of them pretended not to see my father reading to me, which made it even more strange. I smiled a big smile, but kept my eyes on the book. Normally, even a glance at the text on my part made my father self-conscious. This time, however, he didn't say anything. He let me stare right at the words he was reading, and when he finished, he closed the book and got into the car quickly and quietly.

To my surprise, we had an understanding. He knew that at least for one moment in time, I was embarrassed of The Streak. And for that, more than anything that had happened that night, I was ashamed.

CHAPTER TWENTY-THREE

Day 2,986

He could not play the game without hope; could not play the game without a dream.

—Gary Paulsen, *Hatchet*

Did you see a ring?"

"No, she had her hands in the dough. I couldn't just ask her to take them out."

"You could have tried to shake her hand."

"Geezle Pete, Lovie! I think you're right again. Should we go back in?"

"No, now it will be obvious."

"What if I act like I just remembered I wanted a cinnamon bun?"

"There's already one in the bag, I think."

"You think! Is there or isn't there? Check!"

"There is. There are two, actually."

"Geezle Pete."

"Wait, I think she's heading toward the window. I can probably get a good look. Stand here and act like you're eating your doughnut."

I had more wing-woman experience than most teenage girls. Sometimes a single dad needs a hand.

"Why would I *act* like I'm eating a doughnut? Can't I just eat it?"

"There it is. There's a ring."

"A wedding ring?"

"Looks like it. A gold band."

"Geezle peezle. We're dead ducks, Lovie."

There are plenty of things my father does well. He is very skilled at baseball analysis and giving driving directions, and he's even got a pretty strong drawing hand. But he's never been particularly good, or perhaps the word is *lucky*, when it comes to dating.

That's not to say, of course, that he has not dated. At some point in his life, he must have dated my mother. And then he was single, and then he started dating Lee.

Lee was a thin woman with curly blonde hair and kite-like shoulders. She was in the audience for the matinee of one of my performances in high school and came up to me afterward to say hello.

"You probably don't remember me," she began.

I didn't.

"Of course I do! You're, hmm..."

"Lee! I used to work with your dad. Well I just wanted to let you know what a great job you did up there!"

She had a nice smile and smelled like a home.

"Thank you! Thank you for coming. I will tell my dad I saw you."

"Yes, please do!"

Even though I liked her, I forgot.

A few weeks later, my father said that he was going out for the evening with Lee.

"Oh! She came to my play. I was supposed to tell you."

"I know. She sent me a letter."

"A letter? Saying what?"

"That she's got the hots for me."

"It did not say that!"

"If it didn't come right out and say it, that was still the general idea."

It had never even occurred to me that my father might want to date. He hadn't mentioned women, even in passing, other than noting our superior mental capacity. In what I later learned was an effort to stabilize our home and make it clear that my sister and I were his real priorities, my father had gone six years without a woman in his life. Before this very moment, I had not considered how strange that was. When he came home later that night, smiling and whistling as he made himself a cup of tea, I wondered how long he'd been thinking about this moment. I wondered if he'd had butterflies.

Two weeks later, I asked for permission to go on my first date.

"Can I go to the boardwalk with Ben?" I whispered

through the crack in his door, as he was just waking up from his nap (and at his most relaxed).

"Who else will be there?"

"No one."

He closed his eyes for a minute, and I thought he was going back to sleep. Then, without opening them, he said, "If you plan to be out late, we're going to need to read first."

As I got dressed for the big night, I considered the possibility that I might come back whistling too. I did, and by the end of that summer we were both in relationships.

When we had dates on the same night, we would compare notes as we got ready. This generally consisted of him telling me what great shape he was in and how every outfit looked good on him, though some looked better than others. Then I would ask him what he thought of my outfit, and he would make a pained look and comment on the color or the fabric. If there was time, he would usually make me hand over the entire ensemble so he could iron it, because he was very passionate about well-ironed clothes.

"It only takes a few minutes, and you go from looking like a horribly wrinkled monkey warrior to a real class act."

I have never figured out who these monkey warriors are or what harrowing experience left them with bodily wrinkles, but having a father who loves to iron has always been advantageous.

We both stayed in our respective relationships for a few years, and I really came to care for Lee. She had children of her own and took me under her wing without even having to think about it, making me Easter baskets, baking on my birthday, and accompanying my father to any event that involved cheering me on. She even seemed to get along with my mother. We were starting to feel like a lopsided but somehow logical, happy family. And then, no one really understood what happened.

I was sitting in the dining room a few weeks before my senior prom. I had on the Phillies game, which my father was attending in person, and I also had on every light in the house. Being home alone still made me nervous. I thought every noise was someone creeping onto our front porch, so I nearly ran for the phone when I noticed that someone actually *was*. When I realized that it was Lee, I sighed, and laughed, and went to the door to let her in. But when I got there, she was already backing out of the driveway. On the porch was an early graduation present to me, a gorgeous forest-green set of luggage with a lovely, heartfelt card. Next to the luggage, in a neat and tidy pile, every gift my father had ever given her looked up at me regretfully.

"I just don't understand," I heard him say on the phone that night.

There was a pause, and then, "Are you sure?"

Another pause, this time shorter.

"Well, I'm not going to beg you," he said, and he hung up the phone.

After two years, the conversation lasted less than thirty seconds. He was blindsided.

He seemed upset for a day or two, but then he began repeating, like a boxer with a mantra, the same general phrases: "She was a great find but I am a great find, too. I will move on and find better. If she doesn't want me, the heck with it. Someone else will jump at the chance. I am in great shape."

He dated, and quickly realized that though women were available and interested, he would be starting all over again. He missed the comfort of his relationship. He missed Lee.

So he spent a few months trying to find out what had happened between them. He tried leaving her notes, and making small gestures, and letting her know that she was still on his mind. There was even one golden moment when a friend said that she'd seen a photo on Lee's desk of her with my father, long after the breakup. Buoyed with hope, my father called her for the first time in months. It turned out the photo was of another white-haired man.

He went back to dating, but since he hadn't done it in years (Lee had pursued him, and there had been no one between her and my mother) he was out of practice. At first, his standards were too high—he was looking for someone in great shape, who could cook and wanted to be a part of the family, and who loved to travel and sometimes listen to Elvis. He was looking for Lee. Even when I convinced him to lower his standards a bit, though, his luck didn't improve much.

"So how was that blind date?" I asked one morning, as I was organizing my things into piles for my senior class trip. He had gone on a few in the past month, but none was quite what he'd been hoping for.

"Lousy," he said, sitting on his bed and rubbing his feet.

"You can sum it up in one word? Was it really that bad?"

"I walked up to the restaurant, and there was this man who looked exactly like George Washington outside, waving to someone. When I got closer I realized that he was waving to me. When I got even closer, I realized he was a she."

I let air out between my teeth.

"Well, that's a rough start, I'll admit, but you can't keep judging these women by their looks. Not everyone is as passionate about exercise as you are, you know."

"She chewed with her mouth open, cursed like a sailor, and *bragged* that the only thing she reads for pleasure is the funny pages. Are my standards still too high?"

After months, and then years, of similar stories, I became my father's personal salesman. I had no choice, as far as I could see—I wanted him to be happy, and he couldn't seem to figure it out on his own. I started off tentatively ("It's funny, my father laughs the same way!"), but gained momentum quickly.

"You know," I said to an attractive, middle-aged woman helping me find my shoe size at a local department store, "you really should wear your ring, if you're married."

She looked confused.

"But I'm not married," she said.

"Oh! Well you know, actually, neither is my father. I wonder what else you two might have in common!"

My tactics might be a bit too direct, because as of this writing, he has yet to find anyone. He goes through moments of optimism and times of frustration, but he is still looking, which is all I can ask for. As long as he still wakes up in the morning believing that the woman for him is out there, I think he comes closer to finding her. It just hasn't happened yet.

But it has to, and not because I want it to—my father has to find someone because it's impossible that he wouldn't. We noticed a pattern over the course of The Streak, books about mothers who left the family and fathers or grandfathers who had to try to piece things back together. These male characters were always sad, mopey creatures, curling up in their bedrooms and hiding from the world. My father was never that man, and we laughed at these stories. What had inspired these authors to write such unrealistic tales? Weren't there men anywhere like my father? Men who woke up excited about the day, optimistic about raising children alone, full of humor and life? In all of The Streak, we never found a character who looked at his situation the way my father did, eager to find someone but unafraid to raise his daughters as a single man.

In the books we read, even those sad, unfamiliar men often found someone. Some lovely woman wandered in, made the man laugh for the first time in years, and brought him back to life. My father was full of life, but this woman never came. I can't even say for sure if the stories gave him hope. But we kept reading them, so something must have stuck. I know that the right woman is out there, maybe reading this book and wondering why she's never met a man like my father.

If I met her, I would remind her that *no one* is like him. Not even close.

CHAPTER TWENTY-FOUR

Day 3,156

The world itself was a whirligig, its myriad parts invisibly linked, the hidden crankshafts and connecting rods carrying motion across the globe and over the centuries.
—Paul Fleischman, *Whirligig*

I sat at the intersection for quite some time, waiting to cross over to the other side. I was a terrified new driver with almost no desire to use my freshly minted license. My friend had been able to convince me to visit him only because his house was within walking distance of mine. But just as I was heading out the door it started raining, and I knew I'd have to drive.

"Be careful crossing the highway," my father had called, as I grabbed the car keys from his nightstand. "There'll be a lot of shore traffic today. Are you sure you don't want me to drive you?"

I said no as I thought yes and now, waiting and waiting and waiting for even a small gap in the endless line of cars, I wanted to turn back and take him up on the offer. But there were three cars behind me already, and there was nowhere to turn around. I tried to give them an apologetic look in my mirrors.

Then the break came, wonderfully large and roomy, big enough for myself and every car behind me. I put my foot on the accelerator. Nothing happened. I pressed harder. Still nothing. I remembered, suddenly horrified, that this had happened as I was pulling out of the driveway, too. There I had stopped, turned off the car and restarted it, and tried again. That time there were no problems. I'd thought about going inside to tell my dad, but I figured whatever the problem was, it was probably something I'd forgotten to do, something small and silly. Now I knew that it was the car, and I was stuck. Nowhere to turn around, no way to back up, sitting at the edge of an intersection in a car that wouldn't go. I decided I needed to calm down and think for a minute, try not to panic, try not to look at the cars around me.

What was that? I felt a tug in my stomach I initially thought was nerves, and then I noticed that I was moving. Not the kind of slow, rolling movement that should have taken time to register. I was being yanked forward at top speed into oncoming traffic faster than I knew cars could move, like being towed by a race car. Everything lurched forward, I was thrown against the steering wheel; I realized, too late, that I'd never taken my foot off the gas when I stopped to think. Somehow, after two or three minutes, the car had registered my request to speed up and move forward, and granted it tenfold. I couldn't think to put my foot on the brake; it was as though it wasn't actually happening to me. I was just watching myself, and the car, careen into traffic. Something hit my bumper. My car spun onto someone's lawn. It landed on the street again, heading back to the highway. The car made screaming sounds, or maybe that was me. I smashed into a fire hydrant and smelled smoke all around me.

I looked up. The thing that had hit my bumper must have been another car, because there one was, stranded on the highway, hood dented and crinkled like an origami project. I heard sirens and people yelling, the smoke got thicker, the rain came down harder. My head was pounding. Trucks pulled up all around me, well, us. There was someone familiar behind the wheel of the other car, a woman with soft round cheeks and short brown hair. My mother. She wasn't looking at me. They were coming to take her away again.

In the dizziness and confusion, the lights and sounds around me, the face of the stranger in the other car had changed to that of my mother. I slouched over my steering wheel and closed my eyes, trying to separate the moment from the memory. They were blending together dangerously; I wondered if I was dreaming, or falling asleep.

I was nine years old. I got up to use the bathroom in the middle of the night, which I never do, and heard sirens in the distance, moaning to each other in a language I sort of thought I understood. There was another moaning, closer, inside the house. I ran downstairs and found my mother on the kitchen floor, sprawled out like a doll someone had suddenly dropped to go do something else. There were little dots all around her, some sort of white bug all over the counters and crawling down onto the floor. Some of the bugs were on her, on her shirt and in her hands. I waited for my eyes to adjust to the light and realized that they were pills, little white circles and ovals, sprinkled all over. I'd seen the pills before, she took them for everything from depression to a blister, but never in this quantity. The phone was on the floor, I could hear my godmother's voice on the other end.

"Hello?" I said cautiously into the mouthpiece.

My mother looked up, thinking I was talking to her. Her eyes were red and tired looking, but also distant and, in an odd way, very relaxed. She looked like she was about to smile and say something to me, but then her face clouded over and she started crying, mumbling something as she sobbed.

"Sweetheart!" my godmother said with surprise. "Okay, this is good. Listen, your mom is going to be okay. There's an ambulance on the way. You should see flashing lights any minute. Be ready at the door and let them in when they come. Are you all right? Do you understand what's going on?"

"Yes," I said, though I wasn't sure which part I was responding to. I couldn't tell if I was all right. I was barely awake. And I wasn't sure what was going on. My mother had taken some pills, and spilled some, and now she was taking a nap on the kitchen floor, only she was very upset about it. I went upstairs to wake up my sister, because she would know what to do. I explained what was going on, as much as I could. After a few words she heard the sirens and jumped out of bed.

"*Dad!*" she screamed into the dark. "Dad, wake up!"

We got in our car to follow the ambulance. It made everything on the road red and white, like Christmas lights but more desperate. The moaning of the sirens continued. Sometimes I thought it was my mother, but it couldn't have been, because she was inside the truck and the doors were closed. People were moving around in there with her; I could see them whenever we got close enough, picking up things and gesturing to each other. I was the one who let them in when they came to the door and they had been kind, soft, patient. Now they looked angry, their faces taut and tense, arms swinging wildly in the air and then landing firmly on some object, which they carried to my mother's side. I couldn't actually see my mother, but I knew she was there, on some sort of mat just below the window, tucked away out of sight. They probably didn't want anyone to see her crying. She made awful faces when she cried, scrunching up her cheeks and getting her face all red. My crying face would have looked even worse if I'd been crying, but the swirling, flashing lights brought a strange sense of calm over me. No one would sleep through this; my mother would not just close her eyes and go away. How could she? The sound was deafening, the moaning became screeching, and I wanted it to get louder and louder, to keep us all awake. Especially my mother, who was trying to go to sleep on that cot in that truck, but they wouldn't let her. They kept the lights on and kept the sirens screaming and we all got to the hospital awake.

I opened my eyes wide for a second. I was in my car. People were running toward me, all around me there was shouting. The rain was coming down harder. I let my eyelids drop.

I stayed awake forever in the waiting room, or so it felt. It was much harder once we got there. Inside the hospital it was quiet. People were whispering because the patients were trying to sleep. Some of the lights were out, and there was a TV in the waiting room softly playing infomercials, barely daring to raise its voice even when it made its most emphatic points. I couldn't keep my head up. I let it fall on my father's shoulder for a while, but then they called us in to see her. I had to wake up.

She was behind a bright white shower curtain, lying on a bed that had lots of tubes coming out of it. There was a pitcher of ice and some cups beside her, but I didn't see any water. She was asleep, but they seemed to think it was all right. They mentioned to my father, in even softer whispers, that they'd had to use charcoal. I wondered if they had started a fire to keep her warm. But no, it was already awfully warm in the room. Maybe they had used the charcoal to draw her picture, like in art class. They might need to remember what she looked like, so they'd know if anything changed. I wondered if my father had a picture of her in his wallet the way people sometimes do, one that he could give to them. I knew he didn't, though.

When we came back later she was awake, or pretending to be. Her eyes were open and she was saying things, but none of them made sense. She was telling my sister that all of this fuss had been because of her, saying that a fight they'd gotten in had left my mother crying and crying and crying like I'd found her. But that wasn't it at all. As I'd gone up to bed that night, I'd seen her frantically writing an e-mail to the man she'd been talking to the most. I recognized his picture in the corner of the screen. Fifteen minutes later she was sobbing and writing frantically back to him. Something he said arrived a moment later and left her wailing even harder. I'd heard all of it in the distance as I tried to fall asleep. What this had to do with my sister I wasn't sure. As far as I could tell, nothing at all. I felt bad that Kath was getting blamed for something she didn't do. I wished my mother would just tell the truth, or the truth as I saw it. But maybe she didn't understand what she was saying, anyway. Her eyes were barely focusing on us.

They told us she'd be better soon. I wondered what that meant. She wasn't sick, as far as I could tell. Not sick like most of the mothers in the books we'd read, or even the ones we would later read, had been. Not sick like Mama in *Esperanza Rising*, or hurt like Amanda Cardinal in *Wish You Well*. She was in a hospital, but she'd done something to go there, and she'd done it quickly—she wasn't even coughing or sneezing the day before. This wasn't like Ramona Quimby getting queasy as she looked at her fruit fly experiment in school, either. It was like nothing we'd read about, and nothing I'd seen. My mother was perfectly well, as far as I could tell, but people were telling me that she would get better.

We left just as the first squeaky streaks of sunlight came out to inspect us. I was sweaty, and the goose bumps on my arms wouldn't go away. I felt strangely secretive about our departure, as though we'd just done something I should try to hide. I wanted to sneak into the car, slink back home, and forget this ever happened. Instead, upon our exit we were greeted instantaneously by another truck pulling up, its lights spinning madly, and that same screaming, screeching moaning tearing through the dawn. I could still hear it. It was getting louder as I remembered it. And there was another noise too, something even closer, but not quite as loud.

I opened my eyes. Someone was tapping on my car window. A man in a raincoat.

"Are you okay?" he asked. "I live in the house right there. I saw everything, you poor thing."

I could barely hear him over the sirens as the fire trucks and ambulances circled us.

I must not have said anything because he kept looking at me and finally asked, "Can you understand me? Are you all right?"

I nodded and got out of the car slowly. The man offered me his coat, but I pushed it away. He offered me his cell phone, which I very much wanted to use, but I was having trouble using my tongue. It felt heavy in my mouth, and my brain seemed to have no control over what it was doing. I managed to run it against the back of my teeth and expected to taste blood. Surprisingly, everything felt fine. No teeth were missing, nothing felt broken or even bruised. Other than a headache and a dizzy, confused feeling, I couldn't notice much of a difference from the way I'd left the house. I reached for the man's cell phone, finally managing to get out the words "Thank you" and smile as warmly as I could without making my headache any worse.

I dialed my house and waited for my father to pick up. As it rang, I saw the woman I'd hit walking into an ambulance. She wasn't hurt, but they wanted to check us both out. And as a precaution, I suppose, they threw on the lights and sounds as they pulled away. That noise. I found myself sobbing without even noticing it at first. My cheeks were wet and hot, I felt tears against the phone and pulled away to try to keep it from getting wet. When my father answered, I was once again struck dumbfounded. I heard his voice, so calm and warm and soothing, and I couldn't speak.

"Hello," he said, always a statement when he answered the phone, never a question.

I sobbed wordlessly, something between a moan and a scream that sounded oddly familiar.

"Hello," he repeated, sounding annoyed but still stating the word, not asking it.

"Daddy," I said, gasping a little to hear the word come out of my mouth. I had never used it much even as a very small child, and probably not at all in ten years. "I crashed the car," I yelled, trying to drown out the sirens and my own crying.

"I'll be right there," he said, without asking where I was. And he was.

We walked home but the noise kept playing. Over and over again, the whirring, sad, sound. I waited for it to die down. When the neighborhood was silent and everyone was asleep, I knew it was coming from me. The sounds of ambulances, and the sounds of my mother, came together in my heartbeat as I tried to fall asleep. But for me, it was the sound of survival. I pulled through, and we'd all pull through, because we were a family of survivors. I was so alive, I couldn't sleep. In the most unexpected ways, I was starting to understand my mother.

To forgive her.

CHAPTER TWENTY-FIVE

Day 3,170

A bud is a flower-to-be. A flower in waiting. Waiting for just the right warmth and care to open up. It's a little fist of love waiting to unfold and be seen by the world. And that's you.
— Christopher Paul Curtis, *Bud, Not Buddy*

Does it have to be a 'gown'? Can't you just wear something you already own?"

"There's a dress code. Plus I'll feel really weird if I'm underdressed. I'll stick out, in a bad way."

"What about a nice skirt and a button-up shirt? Would that fall under the dress code, maybe?"

Single fathers of girls have a lot of tricky issues to face. They deal with puberty, boys, and dating as best they can. I give them, and especially my father, enormous credit for this. My grandmother passed away when I was thirteen. My sister moved out while I was in middle school. My father was too proud to ask his sister for advice. So with relatively little female input, he found his way through the maze of teenage girlhood right beside me, learning to trust me and, eventually, the boys I chose to date. I am proud to say that most of the time, he fully understood what he was doing and made reasonable, logical decisions. I chalk some of this up to all the books we read about young girls. They were almost entirely fiction, but they were usually quite realistic and gave us both great insight into what "normal" girls and "normal" families did. Even with all of our reading, though, some things still absolutely baffled my father. As my senior year of high school came to a close, I realized that prom was one of those things.

My father just didn't understand the hype.

"It's one night!" he kept repeating, whenever he saw the list of things I needed to buy and do.

My list was actually quite modest, compared to most girls I knew: I wanted my hair done, only because I didn't know how to do it myself. I wanted a dress. So far, that was it. I didn't feel the need to bother with shopping for a purse, or jewelry, or even shoes. I was fine with hunting around my closet for something that would come close enough. But things kept popping up.

"Stephanie says I should get my nails done," I mentioned over breakfast one morning shortly before the big night, "but it seems like a waste of money. What do you think?"

"'Done'? What do you mean by 'done'? Painted?"

"Well, that's one option."

"They're too stubbly. You chew on them like you've got the secret to eternal youth in your—what's the white part called? The tip?"

"I could get fake nails, I guess."

"Oh my goodness, no. They look like cat claws, and when the teachers at school get them they make this awful clicking sound whenever they type. It's enough to drive a person batty."

"I wasn't planning on typing very much at prom."

He let air out of the corners of his mouth dramatically.

"Still," he said, "Who would even notice if you had them? In your prom photos, is anyone really going to look at your fingernails?"

I remembered, with a laugh, how my mother's first reaction to my winter formal photos had been: "Why didn't you take the time to get your nails done!"

Though my mother had lots of seemingly logical suggestions on how prom *should* be done, she was having a rough year at work and hadn't offered to contribute financially (my father refused to let me work while I was in school) or drive me around (I hadn't been behind the wheel since my accident), so my father and I were left to puzzle through her advice and complete the adventure on our own. And so far, we were failing in one of the most important categories of all: the dress.

We still hadn't found anything in my price range. I started visiting prom stores with my father and, along with getting a severe case of sticker shock, I noticed that it was something mothers and daughters tended to do together. I felt a pang of jealousy when a friend, whose family was not wealthy by any means, tried on a five-hundred-dollar dress, took one peek out of the dressing room, and was greeted by her mother warmly shouting, "That's it! That's the one. Put the rest away. Call the salesgirl over. We've got our winner."

I picked up another dress from her pile and pointed out the price tag—over two hundred dollars less.

"Well," the mother said, "this is not about money. Sometimes you find it, and you just know. Besides, this is the second most important dress she'll ever wear. And she looks beautiful. So that's good enough for me. This is something a mother does for her daughter."

My mother was interested and supportive, but with my father as my official prom sponsor, things were a little different for me than they were for most of my friends.

"What about this dress you wore when you were in *The Crucible*?" he asked one day, as we sorted through my closet to see if anything I had could possibly be reused. "Everyone said how nice you looked in that, and Kath took all the time to sew it."

"That was a time-period costume. *The Crucible* took place in the late seventeenth century."

"You're the one who always says how much you love vintage."

"I feel like it's not quite the same."

"Now you're just being difficult."

The real problem was that I wanted an actual prom dress. Not a sundress that I could dress up with the right shoes, or a casual dress that might look formal with enough borrowed jewelry. This was my last chance in life to wear a prom dress, and deep down that was what I wanted. I felt guilty. I tried to convince myself that I'd be happy in whatever I wore, that I didn't need to be the belle of the ball. But like the bicycle my father had wanted so many years ago, I started having dreams about it: a poofy, pink, princess dress with enough crinoline to make it stand up straight even when I wasn't wearing it. The bicycle. I finally understood. The dress was something I didn't need. And if I got one, it could have been any old thing. It was silly and unnecessary. But once I'd imagined and dreamed about the dress, anything else felt like running behind while my friends peddled away in front of me.

My father soon wearied of my quest for the perfect dress and brought magazines to the store while I shopped. I'd come out of the dressing room, saleswoman in tow, tiptoeing toward him proudly as I wondered if this might finally be the one.

"Makes you look like all you do all day is think about bass fishing," he'd say, peering for only a moment at me before returning his eyes to his *Newsweek*.

The saleswoman looked awkwardly from my father, to the elegant cream-colored dress with the empire waistline, and finally back to me. She shrugged as though she completely understood where my father was coming from and led me back to the rack.

"I can't take much more of this," my father blurted out during the car ride home. "There are only so many magazines and baseball books in the world. Don't you have friends who are prom shopping? I'll give you whatever money I can. Surprise me. Please, please, surprise me."

The money he gave me was barely enough to buy a nice

pair of jeans, let alone a prom dress. We'd gone back and forth about the price dozens of times. My father was willing to give me what he could, but I couldn't bring myself to tell him a fair price for a dress. After years of living near poverty, it seemed wrong to ask for almost anything, let alone the figures some of my friends' parents were happily forking over. I kept my estimates low, but because my father had never been a teenage girl, they still seemed high to him. Every time I left the house on my hunt, I expected to come home empty-handed. There was nothing, not even the simplest gown, in my price range at most prom stores. But still, in the back of my mind, the dream dress floated around, taunting me and whirling its fluffy layers. It wasn't real. It would never be real, for me.

I knew it the moment I saw it. My friend and I pulled up in front of a thrift store and there, smiling down at me from a third-floor window, was a ballerina-pink, poofy, unquestionably made-for-prom dress. I didn't say anything. I was afraid if I called out, someone else on the street might run in ahead of me, dash up the stairs, and take the dress before I could get to it. So I kept my mouth closed and my head down as I made my way toward it in a trance-like state, like a bug magnetized to a streetlight. I picked it up and held it in my hands. It felt heavy, and still soft, and just right. I looked at the size. It was mine exactly. I looked at the price. It was fifteen dollars more than I had. Even used, I didn't have enough for my dream dress. I tried it on anyway, to convince myself it wouldn't have really looked good. I was right—it didn't look good. It looked breathtaking. Just as I was about to take it off, a saleswoman approached me. She was pointing at something and reaching for one of the layers of crinoline.

"Oh my dear," she said, "I'm so sorry, I didn't realize this was torn. What a pity, hmm."

She held it up to show me, but it looked no different to me than any of the other layers.

"I don't see what you're talking about," I said honestly, putting on my glasses to check.

"What a dear," the woman said with a smile. "You're too kind. Well I certainly can't sell you a damaged dress at that price, now can I? Hmm, how 'bout we take off...Does fifteen dollars sound fair?"

All I could do was nod and uncurl my hand to give her the sweaty wad of cash. During the ride home, I hugged the dress to me tightly and smiled until my dimples hurt.

"I'm almost ready!" I yelled back, as my father called for me for the fourth or fifth time in ten minutes. "But if you want to be surprised, then you can't come charging in here!"

"You're starting to make me nervous!" he yelled. "That boy's expecting you any minute!"

That boy was our neighbor Ryan, a friend I'd had since I was thirteen years old.

"I'm just putting on the finishing touches," I said, adding a necklace that had belonged to my grandmother. I smoothed my hair a few times in the mirror and walked into my father's room.

"Surprise!" I said, as he saw the dress, and my updo, and even the catlike fake nails for the first time.

He looked at me for a long time, and I was afraid he was going to say that I had wasted his money. I was afraid he still didn't "get" prom. I stood up straight so he could see the dress's hand-done embroidery, falling gracefully into the soft pink layers of fluff.

"Well," he said, lowering his eyes and hushing his voice, "you are certainly something else."

When you've spent months preparing for an event, vague answers aren't quite good enough.

"Do you like it?" I asked, fanning the many skirts into a wide curtsy.

"Lovie," he said, "you have never looked so beautiful."

It was a word I'd never heard him use to describe a person. A painting, a house, a lake, maybe. But even though he was always quick to give a compliment, this word must have been put on reserve. He was waiting for some big day to use it. My face was warm as I beamed up at him.

"Now hurry up," he said. "You've been making me a nervous wreck!"

He patted my usual spot on his bed, and I crawled under the covers beside him.

"Watch out!" he yelled as he noticed my updo was about to collide with the headboard. He slid a pillow under my head and eased me down onto it, careful not to let a single hair fall out of place.

Because prom would go until midnight and a friend was having a campfire afterward, we had to do our reading beforehand. My preparations had taken a lot of time, and this was the only time in the day that we were both free. And so, at eighteen years old, in my full prom attire, I nestled up next to my father to hear a chapter from *The Old Curiosity Shop* just before my date arrived.

"When we last left off...," my father began, as he summarized the previous chapter.

I thought I heard him say, *When we last left off: You were nine years old. You chewed your hair when you were nervous. You hated boys and dresses. I was terrified to be a single father.*

He didn't actually say that, though. He just summarized the last chapter, as he always did, and moved on to the next. In that way, our 3,170th night of reading wasn't really that different from our first.

CHAPTER TWENTY-SIX

Day 3,218

If this road goes in, it must come out . . . and as the Emerald City is at the other end of the road, we must go wherever it leads us.

—L. Frank Baum, *The Wonderful Wizard of Oz*

We knew the day was coming. There was no way around it. We'd talked it over and decided that The Streak had to end when I went to college. If not then, when? Would I call him every night, between exams and club meetings, and hope that I was catching him while he was free but before he went to sleep? We'd run up legendary phone bills and every night would be a gamble—would we get in touch? What if he left the phone off of the hook? What if the power went off during a storm? More than anything, though, it wasn't how we wanted The Streak to be. It would make it a chore instead of a joy. The Streak was about spending time together and taking the stress out of a hectic day—not adding more to it.

We were supposed to sit together and appreciate just being in the same room, working our way through a piece of literature. It wouldn't be the same after I left for college. No, it had to end. Once I got my orientation packet, we knew the date: The Streak would end on September 2, 2006. I was hoping for a bright sunny day, maybe even a rainbow off in the distance.

The day came. Tropical Storm Ernesto hit the East Coast with a roar of whipping winds and endless rain. My mother, father, and I piled into the van, and I drove. I had all the usual jitters; I wondered what my roommate would be like, and if my room would be big enough. I wondered if the pink and patchwork comforter set I'd picked out for my bed would look childish. I worried that I wouldn't be able to keep up with college-level math classes. But something bigger was also on my mind.

I was thankfully distracted when we arrived in the worst of the rain and found, to our dismay, that the dorm was at the top of a large flight of stairs. We lugged up my television, and my computer, and my heavy mattress pad. Everything was soaked, including us. I greeted my suite-mates for the first time with hair stuck to my face and my jeans dripping on the tiled floor. Little puddles formed wherever I stood for an extended period of time. When the last of my things came in, it was time.

We looked for a spot. I'd wanted to read outside, and I had pictured it in detail. We'd find a sunny spot a couple hundred yards from my dorm, some place where the grass was tall and green from a lack of foot traffic. I had even seen the perfect place as we were unloading the van, but the rain was getting heavier, and everything outside was becoming one muddy puddle. I suggested we read in my dorm room, where I could lie on the tiny bed while my father sat at my desk, but he dismissed the idea. That space, he said, was too full of boxes. It felt cluttered and tight, and even with the door closed you could hear people coming and going, dragging beds across floors and shouting out the window to their new friends. It wasn't the way to end things, not at all. I agreed, but the problem was, there was no way to end things. Nothing would ever feel quite right. I would rather have searched and searched forever than finally sat down in a spot and said, *This is it. Here is where we will end it.*

So we searched. We walked through my building looking for nooks and crannies, but everything was exposed—there was no privacy anywhere. Then we discovered the tunnels. My dorm was apparently connected to other dorms in the quad by a series of long and winding underground hallways. They led to a small lounge, which, I was amazed to find, already had people in it. Someone had even found a use for the laundry room already, and one machine was clattering loudly. Nothing down here would be of use to us. We were headed back for ground level when my father stopped me on the stairs.

"This will do," he said, sitting down and pulling the book out of his jacket.

"What will? This hallway? Where are you suggesting we read?"

"Right here. On these steps. You can't hear anyone from here."

"But we're on steps! What if someone wants to come down to the basement? It's cold and damp down here. And there's barely any light!" I rattled off my protests as quickly as I could think of them. The only light came from an Exit sign with two large white bulbs beside it. It gave the place a sad, abandoned feel. The hallway echoed a little when we talked. This couldn't be it.

"I'm tired of looking around," he said. "And we're never going to be happy with anywhere."

"I would have been happy with a little grassy hill in the sunshine. Should we wait and see if the rain stops? We could get something to eat and give it a couple of hours."

"It's a tropical storm, Lovie. I don't think it's just going to clear up like that. It'll rain for days."

"I'm not ready," I said, sitting down beside him even as I said it.

"I know. It's just something we've got to do. We'll never be ready."

I sighed. From beneath my hooded jacket, I pulled out a small, worn face. The Raggedy Ann doll my father had gotten me when I was four years old had been a faithful follower of the reading streak. Now, at fourteen years old, her skin was grayish and one of her eyebrows had unraveled. There was a black dot on her face from a marker drawing I made in my bed one night. Her dress, which we'd replaced several times, was faded in the spot where I'd always put my head while my father read to me. She smiled up at me through the loose red yarn surrounding her face and I tried to smile back at her.

"Should we do this?" I said to her, but my father was the one to respond.

"Not really any way around it, is there?" he said.

He put his hand on the cover of the book as though swearing in on the Bible. *The Wonderful Wizard of Oz* was our compromise, since we couldn't agree on which Oz book we'd been reading when we started The Streak. This wasn't it, but it was symbolic to us: the first Oz book. The one that had started it all. In this book, Dorothy wouldn't even meet my namesake Ozma yet. She had no idea what was in store for her. But we knew. We knew how it ended, but we read like we didn't.

We read like we always did. My father and I, together, sharing words that weren't our own but were still a part of our secret language. His voice was calm, deeper than usual, round and soothing. I listened with my arms around my knees. Raggedy Ann was propped up between us, and she was listening, too. He read with a slow confidence that made the first chapter last longer than it probably did the first, second, and third times we'd read this book. He must have been rehearsing for quite some time, or maybe he was just remembering from years gone by, because he barely seemed to be looking at the page. I tried to soak it all up and not think about the future. It wouldn't be this way in ten minutes. In ten minutes, I would be a college student and he would be on his way home without me for the first time. But then, right then, at that very moment, I was Lovie and he was Dad and we were doing what we always did, what we always had done for as long as I could remember. I saw that we were approaching the end, that the first chapter, which he'd marked off with a paper clip, was getting smaller and smaller. When we got to the page with the paper clip, my eyes started to water. I heard a change in my father's voice, he got even slower but it was inevitable. Three thousand two hundred and eighteen nights and days left us here. I knew what came next.

We turned the page.

CHAPTER TWENTY-SEVEN

I'm not running away.
—Jerry Spinelli, *Maniac Magee*

I entered college as, appropriately enough for the daughter of The Streak, an English major. Although The Streak was over and I no longer lived at home, my father and I still found ways to spend time together. When I came home for a weekend, our days were piled high with activities in the Philadelphia area, visiting our old stomping grounds. Had I known the challenges we were about to face in the name of reading, I might have appreciated those days more. They were peaceful. My father was happy. But the conversation we had one particular summer day seems, in an eerie way, like foreshadowing. It was as though my father knew all along what was ahead of him—a fight for the thing he loved almost as much as he loved his own children.

"You know how the water from the bathroom sink always tastes better than the water from the kitchen sink?"

I was surprised that my sister remembered this because now that I was in college, she hadn't lived at the house in four or five years.

"I don't think it really does," I said, though I knew what she was talking about.

"Yes, exactly, that's my point. That's what this mountain was to him. It was the water from the bathroom sink, which you always think tastes better because we don't keep cups in the bathroom. You have to stick your head under the spigot. It's about the challenge. Which is a very selfish reason to risk your life, if you ask me."

"I agree, I think. I don't get the part about the spigot. But I agree with that last bit."

My father, sister (who was, to my excitement, home for the weekend), and I had gone to the Franklin Institute to see an IMAX film and we were now discussing the movie on our way back to the car. My new boyfriend Dan was tagging along, looking as out of place as he was feeling with my still-unfamiliar-to-him family. The movie was about a man who climbed a mountain in Switzerland to prove a point. At least, that was how I saw it. But my father kept saying, "It's something he had to do."

"How is this something he had to do at all?" I argued. "His dad died climbing that same mountain. Half of the movie was about how hard it was for this man to live without a father. And now, his daughter is the *same age* he was when he lost his dad, and he's still going up? He's choosing to abandon her."

"Selfish," my sister repeated.

We nodded our heads in unison.

I sometimes point when I am making an argument, and this time I found myself accidentally pointing at Dan as I spoke. He smirked at my finger and steered it away from his face. I gave him a pat on the back to ensure him I meant no harm. But after I put my hand back in my pocket, I pulled it right out again, this time intentionally pointing at Dan. He had to weigh in.

"Yeah," Dan said in a low voice, not quite comfortable joining a family argument. "I think your dad is right. It's just something he had to do, man."

Dan used the word *man* when he was trying to turn his sentence into a punch line. But I wasn't going to be distracted.

"Lovie," my father said, "sometimes things challenge you, and you know you will never be able to move on with your life until you meet the challenge. You need to prove it to yourself."

My father is far more competitive than most. Once, I tried to convince him to start playing Scrabble with me. I set up the board, taught him the directions, and walked him step-by-step through a few scenarios. For the first ten or fifteen minutes of our inaugural game, he did nothing but tell me how much fun he was having, and what a great educational tool the game was, and how much he hoped we could incorporate a few games into our weekly routines. Fifty minutes later, when I'd beaten him by only forty or fifty points, he made me put the game away and told me to never even suggest playing again. He is just as competitive with himself, pushing himself to walk just a little bit faster or lose just a little bit more weight or haggle a price down by just a dollar or two more at a yard sale. This certainly skewed his view a bit.

"I don't think most people look at life as one big contest, Dad. And even if they did, why would you enter a contest where the grand prize is getting to the top of a cold mountain and second place might involve plunging thousands of feet to your death?"

"And there his wife and daughter were," my sister added, "staying in a cabin at the foot of the mountain, watching their lunatic husband and dad climb a mountain for no good reason."

"I think I gave a perfectly good reason."

"Dad," I said, trying to end the argument without backing down from my point, "let me ask you this: would you have done what he did if Kath and I were little kids waiting for you at the bottom of the mountain, holding our breath and crossing our fingers?"

My sister and I stared, waiting tensely for his response, but knowing what to expect.

"Of course I would," he said calmly and without pause.

This was not what we'd expected. Dan coughed into his sleeve and fell behind to, ostensibly, stop at a water fountain. He took long, slow sips and punctuated each with a deep breath to allow my sister and me time in semiprivate to grill our father.

"What are you thinking?"

My sister stepped away from my father as she said this and gave him a disgusted look, as though he had just revealed he had been bathing in human blood instead of water for the past few weeks.

"Those are some pretty skewed priorities," I said, also backing away. Coming from a man whom I have always considered the most dedicated father on Earth, these statements were shocking.

"Sometimes," my dad said, "there are things a person has to do before they can do anything else. This man couldn't be a good parent until he conquered his fears. How could he tell his daughter not to be afraid of ghosts or the dark or the decaying corpse of a former president"—here he looked at me and smiled—"if he was lying in bed at night, shaking like a leaf thinking about the thing that scares him? There are things you have to do. Some things come even before your family, because if you don't deal with them, you can't take care of your family."

Dan was nodding with his eyebrows raised.

"That makes a lot of sense, actually," he said.

I shot him a look that I thought made it perfectly clear his commentary was unwelcome if he wasn't going to agree with me, but he must have misinterpreted because he continued.

"I can't imagine what that thing would be, for me. But if I had a kid, and something was really distracting me, how could I be a good dad? I guess I couldn't."

"More than distracting," my dad elaborated. "This was taking over his life. It's no different than having a drug problem or a gambling addiction. If it's all you can think about, you need to beat it so you can move on and be a better parent."

What he was saying must have entered through a different ear this time because now it stuck. It was obvious, in fact. I still disagreed in this particular case, but it made sense—in order to be a better parent, you had to be a better person, and that could mean facing some pretty intimidating demons. I realized, feeling suddenly put on the spot, that my father was actually giving my sister and me parenting advice.

"I'm only twenty," I mumbled, turning away from Dan to make it clear I was not trying to make any child-rearing plans with him. Then I felt guilty for excluding him from the conversation, so I poked his arm a few times until he held my hand. Our relationship was highly evolved at this point.

"If your suggestion is to abandon my future children," my sister said, still focusing on the example of the mountain climber, "I don't understand how Egg and I turned out so well."

"No," I said, "that's not it at all. His suggestion is to be your own person before you try to be anything else, because Dad couldn't have been a father if he wasn't at least Jim. Is that it?"

We were sharing a moment, an adult–to–adult conversation about his experiences raising children and his insights for raising mine. It was a conversation we couldn't have had even a year or two ago, while I was still living full-time at the house and fully dependent on his care. He was preparing me for a world that would be, in the not too distant future, mine even more than it was his. My body's strange reaction to coming to a realization, a shiver went down my spine.

"No, Lovie, you've got it all goofed up. I don't know where you get these cracked ideas."

"Really?" I deflated. So much for the moment.

"No, I was just teasing you. Of course that's it. You have to be comfortable with the person you are before you try to raise a bunch of little people. Obviously, the man in the movie wasn't comfortable. His decision wasn't selfish at all. If anything, he was trying to be a better parent. He had to figure himself out. I can't say that I blame the guy."

"Have you ever had to figure yourself out?"

"No," he said, puffing out his chest with pride and pounding it like Tarzan. "I raised two nearly perfect girls, and I always knew who I was."

He raised his arms over his head, miming holding his Styrofoam barbell during his walks through town wearing his various strange hats. The walks, and the stange props, were traditions he'd taken up in the past few years, as much to bewilder fellow Millvillians as to amuse himself. This was to remind us how comfortable he was with himself.

"But," he said, lowering his arms, "if you encounter some bumps on the way, that is probably common. You can't expect everyone to raise children like I can. Just make sure you are reading to them. That certainly won't hurt."

My father has spent the past five or six years collecting books for his grandchildren, to ensure that I will do just that.

As we were about to leave the Franklin Institute that day, we passed through the great rotunda where we had once seen the trapeze artists perform. I nudged Dan and pointed at the ceiling. I'd told him many times the story of how my father had encouraged and even planned for me to join the trapeze man in his act, dangling high in the air with no training and little more than a basic educational background in spelling and addition. To my surprise, my father was thinking about the same thing.

"You know, Dan," he said, "I once brought Lovie here to see a trapeze artist. And she got it in her head to go up, so I went and pretended to talk to the guy, just stood close enough to him that from a distance it might look like we were talking, to make her think I was trying to convince him. Like he would take a child up without even a second thought!"

He laughed a long, hard laugh breathing through his nostrils. I stopped in my tracks.

"You *pretended* to ask him? Does that mean you didn't actually?"

"Are you nuts, Lovie? Can you imagine what that man would have said if I had really come up to him and asked him to let a second grader go flip around in the sky with him? He would have thought I was cracked!"

Again, he started laughing that deep laugh.

"That story makes a lot more sense now," Dan said, eying the domed ceiling and showing a smile.

"Why didn't you ever tell me that? What was the point of that? Why would you convince me that he was practically ready for me to go up if you never actually talked to him?"

Now everyone was laughing except me.

"How does this fit in to your philosophical ideals on raising children?" I persisted, grinding the back of my heel into the ground with embarrassment.

"It doesn't," he said through his laughter. "Sometimes being a parent is just fun."

CHAPTER TWENTY-EIGHT

I have gone over and over my choices—try to temper what I see as the misbegotten policy of putting road miles on children instead of nurturing their minds, or resign in protest.
                                        —Ivan Doig, *The Whistling Season*

My college years rushed along at a surprising pace, and I was glad to be at a school near home. When I was too busy to get away, I called often. Although my father was the only person who ever picked up, his number was saved in my phone not as "Dad" but "Home," like I expected the building itself to answer and tell me how the cats were doing and whether the honeysuckles were blossoming yet. Instead, my father would answer, always happy to hear my voice. I'd tell him about my classes and he'd tell me about his latest and greatest projects in the library. But as my senior year progressed, I noticed that something was wrong. I recalled our conversations just a year or so ago, about the mountain climber in the movie we'd seen. I understood now why my father had defended him. James Brozina was about to climb a mountain of his own.

Changes had been happening at his work for some time before the trouble really began. Computers were moved into the library, and I taught my father how to use them in his lesson plans. He was asked to work in more analyses of stories, so he did. He didn't even complain too much when he was given a second school and his workload was doubled. It meant that he would have over five hundred students, making it difficult to learn their names and personalities, but he took it well. His work was a challenge, but he couldn't help loving it anyway.

Then he came up to have lunch with me one Saturday afternoon during my last semester of college. I could tell something was wrong from the moment I saw him, and it wasn't even because I knew him so well. His shirt was a little wrinkled, which for my father was *extremely* wrinkled, and his face looked like it was drooping. His hair was noticeably thinner, and his skin had a strange, gray tint, as though the blood pulsing under it had suddenly gotten older, or sadder. He'd lost weight. His eyebrows weren't as thick.

"He doesn't want me to read anymore," he said to his pancakes, as we talked over brunch at a diner we'd discovered in Glassboro, down the street from my college. We both always got the same things—pancakes, scrapple, and milk for my father; a BLT, coleslaw, and iced tea for me. We'd gone dozens of times without changing our orders. Today, he forgot to ask for scrapple. I reminded him, but he said he wasn't in the mood for it. His plate looked empty without it.

"Who doesn't?"

"My principal. Well, one of them. He said that I could only read one picture book per class. Five to ten minutes, then on to something else."

"*Five to ten minutes?!* Even a Clifford book takes longer than that, if done well!"

He nodded his head to that emphatically and gulped some milk.

"And the other principal told me, here's the killer—he told me I couldn't read *at all.*"

"*You're kidding me!*"

He shook his head, but he relaxed a little. It occurred to me that he might have come up expecting me to say he was being unreasonable. Maybe others had been saying this.

"What does he want you to do instead?"

He deepened his naturally high voice to do an impression of his principal.

"*THE COMPUTERS!*"

The word made us both wince at the same time. Even though he'd gotten better with them over time, my father did not think computers belonged in the library. Computers belonged in a computer room and books, sacred and worn, belonged in the library. It was a place for reading.

"What's going on? How could this happen at two different schools?"

He stopped eating altogether and passed the rest of his pancakes to me. This was an especially shocking move, as he usually came after my food if I wasn't done by the time he took his last bite.

"Neither of them understand what I'm trying to do.

Mr. Davis ordered hundreds of new books this summer without listening to my suggestions. He said we needed all new, current books because students like new things. He put everything but the picture books, fiction or nonfiction, in storage."

I put up my hand to fight in defense of the collection my father had spent years building, but he raised his eyebrows and gestured his hands in agreement and continued.

"I know! It's absurd! Here's the worst, Lovie—*the library already owned some of the books he ordered!* We had them in hardcover, and he ordered them in paperback. I never order paperbacks because they fall apart in less than a year. He ordered flimsy, paperback versions of books we already had. After all the budget cuts, *that* is how he uses our precious library money. When there are things we really needed, books that the children would have cherished. And where is the collection I spent so many years putting together? In boxes, in the school basement."

I couldn't even imagine what the library must be like now. I tried to picture the happy room my father called his home just a year or two ago. The bookshelves were lined with books that he spent hours hand-selecting, dating from the most current market offerings to out-of-print masterpieces. Some nights during The Streak, I got to hear books that he was trying out for his repertoire and give my opinion. He spent his own money and countless hours at yard sales collecting books and decorations to make the library feel like a comforting, inviting place to read, and he'd succeeded. The walls were covered in hand-done paintings of relaxing scenes. Small fountains sat in the corners of the room, and he plugged them in while the students were reading to create a bit of white noise layered over the classical music he kept on in the background. Instead of overhead lights and classroom chairs, he brought in lamps and upholstered furniture to make students totally comfortable. He put up curtains to block out the sun on hot days and laid decorative rugs over the drab gray carpet. There was even a collection of dolls, available to both boys and girls, for his students to read to quietly. It was heaven for children and books alike, until he came in one morning and found it all in a pile. His request to keep up his decorations and his explanation (that children who enjoyed their time in the library were more likely to read on their own) fell on deaf ears. And now it was happening again. His well-researched methods, which revolved around reading to his students as much as necessary to ignite a love for reading within them, were doubted. The books he'd carefully chosen were replaced.

"The most frustrating part," he summarized as he reached for the check, "is that reading has become irrelevant."

Over the next few weeks, my mind kept wandering to an episode of *The Twilight Zone*. "The Obsolete Man" stars Burgess Meredith as a man put on trial and sentenced to death for the crime of being a librarian. At the time it was written, the world of the episode was sometime in the distant, nebulous future. Now, my father felt as though he were being put on trial, and saw his passion for inspiring children to read become antiquated, quaint—obsolete. He was not about to receive capital punishment, of course, but for a man who had devoted his life to books, watching these items become irrelevant was as close to a death sentence as he had ever come. A few weeks later, when he was told to remove reading from his lesson plans altogether, I couldn't understand how he was even able to get out of bed in the morning.

My father was branded as rebellious and insubordinate because he did what any bibliophile would have done in this situation: he fought back. He began with calm conversations with his principals, asking them why these strange rules were going into effect, and why now. But they didn't seem interested in talking it over. He explained that what he was doing fit the curriculum—buying age-appropriate books and reading to children were both expected on a state level. But as quickly as the words came out of his mouth, they floated away on the breeze, unheard and unheeded. At the school where reading to children in the library was banned, my father moved his classes to the back of the library, turned the lights out, huddled them around him, and read to them in secret.

I couldn't figure out what it was about the reading, or maybe my father, that frustrated these men so much. The main idea, though, seemed to be a desire for change. His principals wanted to make a change, to have the school be different when they left than it was when they came in, and I could respect that. It's hard to imagine leaving a place without making some sort of impact. But to just arbitrarily throw out my father's traditions, like the books that had been thrown out because they were old, seemed wrong. The books, and his lesson plans, lasted as long as they did because they served their purpose. And now, for the sake of modernity, both were being tossed without a second thought. Worst of all, reading was disappearing from the library altogether.

"You have to fight it," I told him one night over the phone.

"Well, I plan to, because it's the right thing to do for the kids. They need to be read to, and they need good books in the library."

"And you should fight for you, too. It's your job and you do it well. People need to respect that you know what you are doing. You were Educator of the Year for the whole city just nine months ago! Doesn't that count for anything? Do you want me to come in and talk to them?"

I knew *that* wasn't a real solution. Still, I could understand why frustrated parents sometimes told off referees or sent angry letters to coaches. No matter how uninvolved you think you should be, it's hard to see someone you love mistreated and do nothing about it.

"I'll call the paper, if you'll let me," I added, hopefully. "I think people will really respond to your story."

"Lovie, I understand that you want to help, and you'd be darn good at it. If you were a lawyer and we could make this a court case, you'd tie everyone up in knots. But I'm sixty-one. Lots of teachers retire at sixty-two. It's not worth the stress to fight it for my own sake. I don't need to defend my job just so that I can stay seven more months. Someone needs to stick up for the kids, and I will, but this can't be about me. It isn't worth it."

To hear my father describe himself, or his position, as "not worth it" made my heart sink, even if he was being logical. Many people would have described all of the money and time he put into his work as "not worth it," but it wasn't a job to him, or even a career. It was his calling.

"You don't *want* to retire at sixty-two! That's not you!" I was fighting back tears and glad that we were talking on the phone, instead of in person, so that he couldn't see my eyes getting red.

"If reading was still the priority, I would work until I couldn't get up the stairs to the library anymore. But if my job is to spend the entire period teaching children about the Internet while perfectly good books sit in storage getting dusty, I can't bring myself to keep going in there."

"But for now, you'll take it to a higher level, for the sake of the kids?"

"For now. For the sake of the kids."

My father scheduled a meeting with some higher-ups in the district. Once a date was set, he devoted all of his free time to researching the benefits of reading aloud. He spent hours collecting articles and studies, printing them out in thick stacks and then searching through them for especially convincing arguments. He reached out to America's most prominent authority on reading aloud, Jim Trelease, a best-selling author on the topic. Trelease responded with suggestions and helpful research ideas. In fact, my father's story moved him to write an essay about the situation (leaving out the name and city, at my father's request) and post it on the homepage of his website. Between my classes I did searches on the benefits of reading aloud to children and sent my father links and suggestions. When the big meeting came, I was feeling confident.

He came up to take me to our favorite diner the next day and looked much better than I had seen him in months. The meeting had gone well—extremely well, in fact. The supervisors in attendance confirmed that reading was indeed a part of the curriculum and that the computers, though important in their own way, were not the point of library time. My father was reluctant to believe that anything would actually come of this meeting, but that made no sense to me. These were district officials! They were on his side! I could barely finish my BLT, but this time it was out of pure excitement. Finally, someone understood.

A week later, my father got a letter about the meeting. He called to read it to me.

"'As we discussed in our meeting,'" he had trouble saying, as though the words were stuck in his mouth, "'you are to read no more than *one* book to each class, lasting no more than five to ten minutes.'"

"It can't possibly say that! We're back where we started! That is not what happened! Is that what happened?"

"No, not at all. I've got my notes from the meeting in front of me. I may have gotten goofed up at some point. I know my hearing is bad, but I couldn't be *that* far off."

"So what are you going to do?"

"What can I do at this point? I've taken it as high up as I can."

"I honestly don't understand what happened. Why did this change?"

"Someone even higher up than the people I spoke to must have disagreed. That's all I can figure. Reading doesn't seem to be too popular right now. Or maybe I'm not too popular."

I knew the latter was impossible—my father is one of the most well-liked men I have ever met, especially on a professional level. Teachers have always been so impressed by his work, they would sometimes give up their free periods to come and sit in the back of his classroom, listening to picture books but enjoying every minute of it.

"You have to talk to someone about this!" I insisted.

"It's not going to do any good."

For the sake of the children, he did send an e-mail: a polite message to one of the people he'd met with asking for some clarification as to why his notes from the meeting differed so much from the letter he'd received. The response was short and curt, saying that he "obviously must have misunderstood" the discussion at the meeting. He sent a follow-up e-mail, and then another, but got no response. For the first time in his life, he visited a doctor about his stress. The doctor strongly suggested that my father was putting his health, and possibly his life, at risk by staying at work. So my father went on medical leave for several months, hoping for some kind of change. Then the call came in from a friend of his—if the rumors were to be believed, every single book had been removed from the library. The room that had so recently been stripped of its homey decor was now stripped of the last thing that made it, by definition, a library.

At the age of sixty-one and in great physical condition aside from the stress, my father retired from the job he had hoped to keep until he could no longer walk up the stairs.

CHAPTER TWENTY-NINE

Once the tugboat takes you out to the ocean liner, you got to get all the way on board. Can't straddle both decks.
—Katherine Paterson, *The Great Gilly Hopkins*

For the first few weeks after my father retired, I came home as often as I could, just to make sure he was all right. Sometimes we didn't even make conversation—I just spent the day sitting beside him, letting him know he was not alone. When he went to bed, I'd talk to him until he fell asleep and then sit in my bedroom, listening to his peaceful breathing until it made me sleepy. At that point, finally relaxed and convinced that things were going to be okay, I'd call my boyfriend. On the phone with him, our problems seemed less stressful. I laughed. I escaped a world where librarians and books didn't matter. I felt like it was okay to start moving, slowly and cautiously, toward something brighter and happier. Because I knew my father would think of something, and mostly because I needed to sleep eventually.

"Just one more story and I'll go to bed," I said, yawning loudly and obviously to make the statement seem more truthful. I was actually starting to get sleepy, but not quite sleepy enough.

"Come on," he said, "You said that before the last story. It's not going to work twice."

"But I really wasn't tired then! And I am now. You're being unreasonable. I can't help it."

"Fine," he sighed, not quite as annoyed as he was trying to sound, "what should it be about?"

"Wait," I whispered, "I think my dad is saying something."

We waited in silence until I realized that he was whistling a song in his sleep. I giggled.

"False alarm."

I took the phone deeper under the covers and put my pillows around my head to create a sound barrier. Without coming out I reached my arm behind my head to turn off my light. The room was cool and dark. The air conditioner kicked on just in time to muffle my voice even more.

"Listen, bud," Dan said, "I am fading fast. Can we keep this one short?"

"No, you said that last night! You said that last night and I went to bed wide awake."

"You got two stories last night and you're getting three tonight! How come I'm always the one who has to tell them? You tell great stories—tell one to me."

"It doesn't count, you're already sleepy. When you can't sleep I'll tell one to you."

Dan made a grumbling noise on the other end of the phone as he thought.

"All right," he began, "Once upon a time, there was a hedgehog."

"What was his name?"

"Worthington."

"Eee," I squealed with delight, "Worthington! That is great."

"And Worthington thought he was very fierce—the fiercest of all beasts, in fact."

"But he was just a hedgehog."

"Don't say it like that! What if I said you were just a girl?"

"I would say you that you are right, but I am a very nice girl. I am small but mighty."

"What happened to keeping this quick?"

"Sorry, okay, so Worthington thought he was the most ferocious of the beasts."

"Yes. But when he had to babysit a group of tiny turtles, he suddenly felt a little less ferocious."

I snuggled up in a ball and let him talk, smiling as Worthington went on a quest to find blueberries for his new friends and gasping when he ran into a large, hairy sloth. Of course the sloth was also looking for blueberries, and they were able to help each other out. Except the sloth was secretly afraid of Worthington's quills—I added that part.

I can't remember when I started asking my boyfriend to tell me bedtime stories regularly. We started dating in college. Time had already passed since The Streak had ended and I had been reading myself to sleep, but it wasn't quite the same.

I wanted to hear someone's voice as I drifted off, someone sitting close by. For most of my life this had been the norm, and I was finding it very hard to adjust to other sounds at bedtime. The radio kept me up; the television made me cranky. Sometimes I could hear people fighting in the hallway outside of my room, but that wasn't quite the comforting thing I was looking for, either. In the spring there were crickets that reminded me of home, but I was on the second floor and could just barely make out their music even when I slid my bed against the window and slept with my head pushed against the screen. I had trouble falling asleep without our tradition.

Dan and my father have very little in common, which is something I like about both of them. They don't remind me of each other, and I don't think they should. Asking Dan to read to me would have been all wrong. But he is an excellent storyteller. Once, when I was upset from an argument with a friend and unable to get myself into any sort of a relaxed state, Dan perched himself on the edge of my bed before he left for the night and put his hand on my forehead, brushing my curls out of my eyes.

"Have you ever wondered," he asked, "if sheep get things caught in their wool?"

I laughed in spite of myself.

"What are you talking about? I guess they do. Maybe branches and leaves and things."

"No, I mean household objects. Towels and spatulas and things. Cat toys. Measuring spoons."

"I've honestly never thought about it," I said, trying to imitate his serious tone but smiling.

"Can you imagine what a pain it must be to have pet sheep? I bet every night before you put them to bed, you have to line them up and shake them out."

"Shake them out?!" I was giddy from the idea and my toes curled under the covers.

"Yes, it simply must be done. There's no way around it. If you don't shake out your sheep before they go to bed, you will lose so many important things. You will spend the rest of your life looking for the remote. And it's not like they like it, either. How would you like to wake up with a paddleball in your sheets? It might sound fun now, but someone could get seriously hurt!"

This thread continued for several nights. Sheep in general turned into three specific sheep: Madeline, Paul, and Gertrude. They lived in my house and tried every night to sneak something past me. It was their goal to someday, somehow, make toast in their bedroom at night. But I knew what they were up to and always remembered to shake them out before they went to bed, because eating in bed would get everything crumby. Then the sheep developed personalities. Gertrude was a troublemaker, always scheming but never planning anything more mischievous than sneaking an extra dessert. Madeline was feminine, outgoing, and fun-loving. She wore lipstick and liked to try on my shoes when I was out of the house. Paul was actually the nicest, only no one would ever know it because his sisters were always framing him. I felt bad for Paul, though, so sometimes he got to be the hero.

Once we had recurring characters, they developed recurring friends. And then like a good TV show, the friends got their own spin-offs, and soon we had a repertoire of thirty or more animals, each with distinct personalities and quirks. They were well-rounded, too; no one was ever all good or all bad. Sometimes they got in fights and sometimes they played awful tricks on each other. It was all highly entertaining, maybe even more than it should have been for two college students.

Life without The Streak was a strange adjustment, and these stories were never quite a substitute. Nothing was the same as being read to by the same person every night without missing a night for years on end. I am content with that— nothing ever has to come close. But at night, when reading to myself was too quiet and my dad was miles away, those stories helped me hold on to a part of my life that I wasn't quite ready to let go of yet, and this lasted all the way through college. And whenever I was home, my father read to me all the time: snippets from the newspaper, portions from a book he was flipping through in the next room. I read to him, too: sections of my writing or e-mails from my sister. We tackled new books even after The Streak ended. A reading family never stops reading. Most nights when I'm home, he'll read in his room and I'll read in my room, and we'll call out funny or thought-provoking passages to each other until he falls asleep. Then I'll grab my cell phone, crawl under the covers, and try to keep my voice down to avoid waking him.

"Hello," I say when Dan answers, "I was wondering what you are going to tell me tonight. Because I think you should know ahead of time that you've got your work cut out for you. I'm not even a little bit tired."

In the room next door I hear my father clear his throat and

roll over. I wonder if I am keeping him awake. I wonder if he feels replaced, hearing someone else tell me my bedtime story. I wonder if it bothers him. Then he flops on his back and snores loudly. I smile.

"Go on," I whisper into the phone. "Just one more story and I'll go to bed."

·

CHAPTER THIRTY

Fawkes is a phoenix, Harry. Phoenixes burst into flames when it is time for them to die and are reborn from the ashes. Watch him.

    —J. K. Rowling, *Harry Potter and the Chamber of Secrets*

My father and I still sulked occasionally. It was the natural thing to do, I think, when someone lost something so important to them—when reading was phased out. But other things came up. The constant snow we'd been getting that winter finally stopped. I had an interview for a program at the University of Pennsylvania, and it gave us something to talk about. Then I got in, and it gave us something to be excited about. We ate meals outside and visited museums. Eventually, we started to feel better.

But my father couldn't just sit at home and adjust to retired life. He enjoyed waking up whenever he wanted, and going back to bed if he felt like it, and taking walks right in the middle of the day when the idea suited him. But he missed reading. So he found a way to do it anyway.

"I'm going to the old folks' home."

"I don't think that's politically correct. Also, you just retired. You are in great shape. There is no reason to put you in a home."

"Obviously I'm fit as a fiddle, you birdhead. I'm going to volunteer there, reading to the old-timers."

For the record, I am not, nor have I ever been to my knowledge, a birdhead.

"What will you read?"

"Picture books."

"To adults?"

"Why not?"

"Won't they be offended?"

"I'll tell them not to be."

"I don't think it works that way."

But as it turns out, it did work exactly that way. My father spent weeks practicing the best of the best books from his personal collection—classics that he'd read to me, like *Merry Christmas, Space Case, Nosy Mrs. Rat, Milo's Hat Trick,* and *Nightgown of the Sullen Moon.* He made plans to visit three retirement homes in one Friday morning. He got up early to practice, and of course, he put on a well-ironed dress shirt and a tie. When he arrived, he explained to them that picture books were what he thought he did best. He wasn't trying to insult them—quite the opposite, actually. He was expressing kindness in the form he knew best, and he hoped they would try to enjoy themselves.

They did. As he described it, they were "mesmerized." They smiled for heroes and cute children and shook their heads disapprovingly when villains appeared. They clapped after every book, and discussed the reading among themselves for a moment before the next book started. My father admitted that a few had fallen asleep at one point or another, but that was to be expected when working with the elderly, and he was not offended. If anything, he decided that he was lulling them into a pleasant late morning nap and making them feel perfectly relaxed. I can testify from some of the close-call, quarter-to-midnight reading sessions that his voice can, at times, have a sonorous quality.

He was extremely pleased with the results of his endeavor, especially since this was a new and unexplored audience for him. He kept up his reading dates every Friday, and the crowds got bigger. A month or so into this routine, he described a scene that I found especially heartwarming:

"I came in to read to my last group of the day, and there was this huge crowd in one room, in rows and rows of chairs, maybe forty or more people. They were all facing the same way, and I assumed they were watching a movie. Well I was pretty disappointed, since this was my usual reading time and they knew I was coming, but I decided I would just have to read to whoever was free. I went up to the front desk to sign in, and the woman told me, 'They're waiting for you.' She pointed at that same room, and I realized that everyone was sitting quietly, looking at me."

That day, my father read to his largest-ever adult audience. The feeling electrified him more than anything else he had done in my recent memory. He couldn't stop raving about the experience, in every phone call and during every car trip, going over again and again the surprise and sudden rush of joy he felt when he realized that all of those people were there to listen to him read. After feeling like his talent was useless for so long, he was reassured and elated to be getting such a great response. He started adding more and more books to his collection, finally getting to try out stories that might have been too difficult for elementary school students. It was his much-needed rebirth, and he practiced his technique now more than ever before.

Then he added a local preschool to his list, and found that, despite what his school district might have led him to believe, children loved being read to just as much as he remembered. Once he thought of volunteering at a hospital to read to children before they underwent surgery, I was almost convinced he'd never have to think of the public school system again.

But inevitably, his mind wandered back to the children he had left behind. After working in a school made up mostly of minorities and almost entirely of children who qualified for free lunches from the state, he always worried about the students who slip through the cracks. A library without books seemed like a nightmarish punishment for students who desperately needed literacy to move on in the world and rise out of poverty. I knew that he couldn't settle with the injustice for too long. His announcement did not come as a surprise.

"I'm running for the school board," he said one day, as though waking up from a long nap.

"After all of that headache, you're going to jump right back into the school system? It's honorable, but I'm not sure that it's smart."

"What happened is not right, and if I can fix it, I am going to."

"What if you can't?"

"Look, Lovie, I'm not saying this won't be difficult. But someone has to step in before reading disappears from schools altogether. Former teachers never run for the board—it's always former administrators. They need my perspective. But I think the most important thing is that they need someone who knows what is going on, and what our students are losing."

I knew all of this before he said it, but I wanted to hear him say it, because I needed to hear the passion in his voice. I was and always will be in his corner, but it was an even better place to be once I realized that he still had some fight left in him.

"You know, you make a pretty convincing argument."

"That's a relief. I think that will come in handy when elections roll around next year."

"Next year? That's a long time."

"So I've got time to prepare."

And so he does. For now, he lives a pretty typical retired life, volunteering and working on projects around the house. He goes grocery shopping on Thursday mornings and listens to baseball on the radio. In my mind, that makes him all the more interesting. He is like a superhero, practicing living a normal life before starting his career as a defender of libraries, books, and the all-important art of reading. When elections come, and the town realizes the threat it is facing, he will fight for what is good and right in the world, and protect us from disaster. But first, he has to practice his cover.

We have a birdbath in our front yard. It's on a little platform that my dad made out of cinder blocks so that he could watch the birds from the living room window. But more often than not, he prefers to be on the porch. He brings a book, and maybe a dish of ice cream, and he sits in a rocking chair. He doesn't actually rock—he tries to stay still so that the birds don't fly away. Sometimes he doesn't even open the book. He rests it on his lap and counts the birds as they come by. He looks like he is waiting for something, because he is. He's waiting for a change. He made a commitment that he still can't seem to shake.

We called it The Reading Streak, but it was really more of a promise. A promise to each other, a promise to ourselves. A promise to always be there and to never give up. It was a promise of hope in hopeless times. It was a promise of comfort when things got uncomfortable. And we kept our promise to each other.

But more than that, it was a promise to the world: a promise to remember the power of the printed word, to take time to cherish it, to protect it at all costs. He promised to explain, to anyone and everyone he meets, the life-changing ability literature can have. He promised to fight for it. So that's what he's doing.

Thirteen years ago, my father made the reading promise to me.

He kept his word.

My father was not the only person to make this promise. I made it, too, just as millions of people have made it around the world. Since books were first created, copied by hand beside glowing firelight, many have recognized them for the treasures they really are. Men and women everywhere have valued and protected these treasures. They may not start a reading streak, but the commitment is still there. There is always time to make the commitment to read and defend reading, and it is a commitment that is always worthwhile. *This is more important now than it has ever been before.* Unfortunately, my father's situation is not unique: day by day, literature is being phased out of our lives and the lives of our children. This is the time to act. This is the time to make a promise.

The Reading Promise

I, _____, promise to read.

I promise to read on my own, in print or on a screen, wherever books appear. I promise to visit fictional worlds and gain new perspectives—to keep an open mind about books, even when the cover is unappealing and the author is unfamiliar. I promise to laugh out loud (especially in public) when the chapter amuses me, and to sob uncontrollably on my bed for hours at a time when my favorite character dies. I promise to look up words when I don't know them, and cities when I can't locate them, and people when I can't remember them. I promise to lose track of time.

I promise to read with _____, if not every night, then whenever I can. I promise to remember that this person is more than my son, daughter, mother, father, sister, brother, aunt, uncle, cousin, landlord, or dog walker; he or she has a mind that, like mine, loves to be used and challenged. I promise to share books however it suits us best, whether we choose to read to each other or simply get together for discussions and homemade baked goods. I promise to appreciate the time we spend together and the literature we meet, even when I am stressed or tired or sunburned (or an awful combination of the three), because books are better when they're shared. I promise to do my best to meet our goal, whether that goal is to read for ten thousand nights or simply to get to know each other better. I promise never to give up on reading, nor let us give up on each other, whether we meet our goal or not.

I promise to support reading in my community of _____ however I can, and everywhere else for that matter. I promise to spread the word about words, whether it's volunteering at my local library or just recommending good books to friends. I promise to speak out if reading is cut from the school curriculum, and to fight for books whenever their value is challenged. I promise to tell everyone I know how reading calms me down, riles me up, makes me think, or helps me get to sleep at night. I promise to read, and read to someone, as long as human thought is still valued and there are still words to be shared.

I promise to be there for books, because I know they will always be there for me.

LIST OF BOOKS FROM
THE READING STREAK

My father and I had no idea what The Streak would become and therefore never made a list of the books we read. Many have been forgotten, but these are the ones we remember.

The Last Treasure by Janet S. Anderson
Mr. Popper's Penguins by Richard and Florence Atwater
The Barn by Avi
Wish You Well by David Baldacci
Harry the Poisonous Centipede by Lynne Reid Banks
Searching for David's Heart by Cherie Bennett
A Gathering of Days by Joan W. Blos
Skeleton Man by Joseph Bruchac
The Secret Garden by Frances Hodgson Burnett
Trouble River by Betsy Byars
The Family under the Bridge by Natalie Savage Carlson
Alice's Adventures in Wonderland and *Through the Looking
    Glass* by Lewis Carroll

Al Capone Does My Shirts by Gennifer Choldenko

Shen of the Sea by Arthur Bowie Chrisman

Murder on the Orient Express and *Ten Little Indians* (Also known by the title *And Then There Were None*) by Agatha Christie

Pinocchio by Carlo Collodi

My Daniel by Pam Conrad

The Wanderer by Sharon Creech

Bud, Not Buddy by Christopher Paul Curtis

James and the Giant Peach, Danny the Champion of the World, and *The Minpins* by Roald Dahl

Because of Winn-Dixie by Kate DiCamillo

Great Expectations, The Pickwick Papers, A Christmas Carol, and *The Old Curiosity Shop* by Charles Dickens

The Whistling Season by Ivan Doig

The Adventures of Sherlock Holmes by Sir Arthur Conan Doyle

Ginger Pye by Eleanor Estes

Tales from Silver Lands by Charles J. Finger

Whirligig and *The Half-A-Moon Inn* by Paul Fleischman

Stone Fox by John Reynolds Gardiner

Pictures of Hollis Woods by Patricia Reilly Giff

The Other Shepards by Adele Griffin

Among the Hidden and *Among the Betrayed* by Margaret Peterson Haddix

Hoot by Carl Hiaasen

The Year of Miss Agnes by Kirkpatrick Hill

Goodbye, Mr. Chips by James Hilton

Indigo by Alice Hoffman

THE READING STREAK BOOK LIST

When Zachary Beaver Came to Town by Kimberly Willis Holt

Stormbreaker, Point Blank, Skeleton Key, Ark Angel, and
    Eagle Strike by Anthony Horowitz

Up a Road Slowly and *Across Five Aprils* by Irene Hunt

The Secret Journey by Peg Kehret

In the Stone Circle by Elizabeth Cody Kimmel

From the Mixed-up Files of Mrs. Basil E. Frankweiler and *The
    View From Saturday* by E. L. Konigsburg

Beyond the Open Door by Andrew Lansdown

The Secret in the Woods by Lois Gladys Leppard

Spy X: The Code by Peter Lerangis

Ella Enchanted by Gail Carson Levine

The Lion, the Witch and the Wardrobe and *The Voyage of the
    Dawn Treader* by C. S. Lewis

The Giver and *Anastasia Krupnik* by Lois Lowry

Journey by Patricia MacLachlan

Be a Perfect Person in Just Three Days by Stephen Manes

The Doll People by Ann M. Martin

Good Night, Maman by Norma Fox Mazer

Winnie-the-Pooh and *The House at Pooh Corner* by A. A. Milne

Thomas Jefferson: A Boy in Colonial Days by Helen A. Monsell

It's Like This, Cat by Emily Neville

Island of the Blue Dolphins by Scott O'Dell

The Great Gilly Hopkins by Katherine Paterson

Hatchet by Gary Paulsen

A Year Down Under by Richard Peck

The Moosepire and *Once Upon a Blue Moose* by Daniel
    Manus Pinkwater

Select short stories and poems by Edgar Allan Poe

Pawns by Willo Davis Roberts

Esperanza Rising by Pam Muñoz Ryan

Missing May and *The Islander* by Cynthia Rylant

Holes by Louis Sachar

The Bears' House by Marilyn Sachs

A Midsummer Night's Dream and *Macbeth* by William
    Shakespeare

Among the Dolls by William Sleator

Cat Running by Zilpha Keatley Snyder

Miracles on Maple Hill by Virginia Sorenson

Maniac Magee and *The Library Card* by Jerry Spinelli

The Mouse of Amherst by Elizabeth Spires

Andy Jackson: Boy Soldier by Augusta Stevenson

Surviving the Applewhites by Stephanie S. Tolan

Banner in the Sky by James Ramsey Ullman

Dicey's Song by Cynthia Voigt

Each Little Bird That Sings and *Love, Ruby Lavender* by
    Deborah Wiles

The Moonlight Man by Betty Ren Wright

The Pigman by Paul Zindel

L. Frank Baum books:

The Wonderful Wizard of Oz

The Marvelous Land of Oz

Ozma of Oz

Dorothy and the Wizard of Oz

The Road to Oz

The Emerald City of Oz

The Patchwork Girl of Oz
Tik-Tok of Oz
The Scarecrow of Oz
Rinkitink in Oz
The Lost Princess of Oz
The Tin Woodman of Oz
The Magic of Oz
Glinda of Oz
Dot and Tot of Merryland
American Fairy Tales
The Master Key: An Electrical Fairy Tale
Mother Goose in Prose
Queen Zixi of Ix
The Sea Fairies
Sky Island
The Enchanted Island of Yew
The Magical Monarch of Mo
Father Goose: His Book
Little Wizard Stories of Oz

Judy Blume books:

Freckle Juice
Tales of a Fourth Grade Nothing
Superfudge
Fudge-a-Mania
Double Fudge
The One in the Middle Is the Green Kangaroo

Ramona books by Beverly Cleary:

Beezus and Ramona
Ramona the Pest
Ramona the Brave
Ramona and Her Father
Ramona and Her Mother
Ramona Quimby, Age 8
Ramona Forever
Ramona's World

Harry Potter books by J. K. Rowling:

Harry Potter and the Sorcerer's Stone
Harry Potter and the Chamber of Secrets
Harry Potter and the Prisoner of Azkaban
Harry Potter and the Goblet of Fire
Harry Potter and the Order of the Phoenix
Harry Potter and the Half-Blood Prince

Encyclopedia Brown books by Donald J. Sobol:

Encyclopedia Brown, Boy Detective
Encyclopedia Brown Strikes Again (aka *Encyclopedia Brown and the Case of the Secret Pitch*)
Encyclopedia Brown Finds the Clues
Encyclopedia Brown Gets His Man
Encyclopedia Brown Solves Them All
Encyclopedia Brown Keeps the Peace

THE READING STREAK BOOK LIST

Encyclopedia Brown Saves the Day
Encyclopedia Brown Tracks Them Down
Encyclopedia Brown Shows the Way
Encyclopedia Brown Takes the Case
Encyclopedia Brown Lends a Hand
Encyclopedia Brown Carries On
Encyclopedia Brown Sets the Pace
Encyclopedia Brown and the Case of the Disgusting Sneakers
Encyclopedia Brown and the Case of the Dead Eagles
Encyclopedia Brown and the Case of the Midnight Visitor
Encyclopedia Brown and the Case of the Mysterious Handprints
Encyclopedia Brown and the Case of the Treasure Hunt